CRAPPIE TACTICS

How, When and Where to Catch More Fish

by Larry Larsen

A LARSEN'S OUTDOOR PUBLISHING BOOK
THE ROWMAN & LITTLEFIELD PUBLISHING GROUP, INC.
Lanham • Chicago • New York • Toronto • Plymouth, UK

Published by
LARSEN'S OUTDOOR PUBLISHING
An imprint of The Rowman & Littlefield Publishing Group, Inc.
4501 Forbes Boulevard, Suite 200, Lanham, Maryland 20706
http://www.rlpgtrade.com

Estover Road, Plymouth PL6 7PY, United Kingdom

Distributed by National Book Network

British Library Cataloguing in Publication Information Available

Library of Congress Cataloging-in-Publication Data Available

Library of Congress 93-79800

ISBN: 978-0-936513-40-9 (paper : alk.paper)

♾™ The paper used in this publication meets the minimum
requirements of American National Standard for Information
Sciences—Permanence of Paper for Printed Library Materials,
ANSI/NISO Z39.48-1992.

Printed in the United States of America

ACKNOWLEDGMENTS

A special thanks to my parents, who like most, taught me how to catch panfish when I was a toddler. At the age of three, I was on a creek bank with canepole in hand trying to keep small bluegill and crappie from stealing my worms and minnows. My most memorable crappie catch came while fishing with my parents on Tuttle Creek Reservoir near Manhattan Kansas about 15 years later. We found the crappie spawning in one foot of water in the back of a small cove and caught one on every cast. We tired of catching the fish which ranged up to two pounds, and I tired of cleaning almost a limit of them. Fortunately, we threw back most of the more than 200 crappie we boated that one afternoon.

Now 30 years later, I still enjoy catching crappie. I think it's one of those things that gets in your blood when you are three years old and you have just caught more and bigger fish than your two year old brother. I owe it all to my parents!

I want to also thank my many fishing friends with whom I've wet a line. There are many, and all were a pleasure to be with.

3

PREFACE

"Crappie Tactics" focuses on when and how to catch America's favorite "Funfish" - the crappie. Productive tactics, lure and bait basics, seasonal strategies, tournament preparation and advanced techniques are presented in this book. There are numerous tips and tricks offered to readers interested in catching more crappie.

Whether it is called speckled perch, Sac-a-lait, papermouth, white perch or any number of other monikers, the fish is found in every state except Alaska. Crappie provides thrills to millions of anglers of all ages and skill levels; this book is dedicated to them.

The information in this text will benefit all anglers, regardless of their skill level. More than 40 line drawings and photos carefully illustrate and detail highly productive tactics.

The tips within each chapter will make a better crappie fisherman of all. The author's proven techniques are applicable to all waters around the country. For anglers who want to learn to be better crappie fishermen and to enjoy their fishing more, "Crappie Tactics" casts in their direction.

In Section I, the book covers "The Basics For Fun". Line, lures, bait, rods and poles, reels, hooks and floats are all reviewed. Seasonal information such as catching crappie during the spawning phase or summer doldrums is highlighted. Release or mounting considerations for giant "speck" are covered also in this section.

In Section II, you will find the top ''Places For Action'' and how to fish each. Finding the good spots, checking out the vegetation, natural and man-made structures and learning to analyze a lake provides vital information for success not found elsewhere. You'll catch more fish after reading this one section alone.

Section III is for those who want to consider some ''Advanced Tactics'', such as using pH to locate crappie or markerology for concentrations of the fish. This section discusses attractants and scent products, tide water fishing opportunities and tournament preparation, among other things. Even an expert should walk away with valuable information from this section.

CONTENTS

Acknowledgments 3
Preface.. 5
About The Author 9
INTRODUCTION 11

SECTION I - The Basics For Fun

Chapter 1
LURE AND BAIT CONSIDERATIONS 13
Chapter 2
THE RIGHT EQUIPMENT 19
Chapter 3
STRIKE DETECTION - HOOKS & BOBBERS 25
Chapter 4
UNTANGLING LINE MESS..................................... 29
Chapter 5
SPAWNING SLABS.. 35
Chapter 6
HOT WEATHER OPPORTUNITIES 43
Chapter 7
RELEASE YOUR TROPHY CATCH? 49
Chapter 8
MOUNT YOUR TROPHY CATCH? 53

SECTION II - Places For Action

Chapter 9
HOW TO FIND GOOD SPOTS 57
Chapter 10
FISHING IN THE GRASS... 61
Chapter 11
'STRUCTURE' YOUR FISHING 67

Chapter 12
UNDER THE PLANKS 73

Chapter 13
DIGGING FOR SPECK ACTION 79

Chapter 14
HOT WATER CRAPPIE 87

Chapter 15
BAYOU BASIN SAC-A-LAIT 93

SECTION III - Advanced Tactics

Chapter 16
ANALYZE THE LAKE 101

Chapter 17
ELECTRONICS STRATEGIES 107

Chapter 18
THE CRAPPIE pHISHING CONCEPT 113

Chapter 19
MARK YOUR HONEY HOLES 121

Chapter 20
MAKING SENSE OF SCENT PRODUCTS 129

Chapter 21
CATCH TIDEWATER CRAPPIE 135

Chapter 22
TOURNAMENT PREPARATION 143

Resource Directory 149
Index 157

ABOUT THE AUTHOR

Larry Larsen is a prolific fishing writer and author and is a frequent contributor on crappie subjects to major outdoor magazines. More than 1,500 of Larsen's articles have appeared in magazines, including Outdoor Life, Sports Afield, Field & Stream, Crappie, Bassin', North American Fisherman, Bass Fishing, Fishing Facts and Fishing Tackle Trade News. His photography has appeared on the covers of many national publications.

The Lakeland, Florida outdoor writer/photographer has now authored 18 books on fishing and contributed chapters to another eight. They include the award-winning BASS SERIES LIBRARY, GUIDE TO FLORIDA BASS WATERS SERIES and others. Larry is president of Larsen's Outdoor Publishing (LOP), the fastest growing publisher of outdoor titles in the country, and a member of the Outdoor Writers Association of America (OWAA), the Southeastern Outdoor Press Association (SEOPA), and the Florida Outdoor Writers Association (FOWA). Complete information on the author's other books and the LOP line of outdoor books can be found in the Resource Directory at the back of this book.

The author is not just a writer who has studied and written about all aspects of fishing for more than 24 years, he is an accomplished angler. As a result, his published works detail proven fish catching methods and special techniques. Larry works with several tackle companies on new lure and techniques development. His analysis of what works and why will help anyone catch more and bigger fish!

INTRODUCTION

America's Favorite Panfish

Specks, as crappie are called in some places, is actually short for speckled perch, a generally-southern misnomer for the black crappie. The crappie, however, is not really a perch at all, but a sunfish, and thus, a relative of the bass and bluegill.

The future of crappie angling looks very bright. Anglers today buy a lot of live bait, such as worms and minnows, because they just want to catch fish. They don't have to go bass fishing, they just go "fish fishing". Crappie and other panfish are popular because they are relatively easy to catch.

One of the factors influencing that future is people trying to get the family unit reestablished. A lot of people in their 40's are now taking their dads out fishing, and they are going after crappie. The population is getting older, the baby-boomers are getting older, and it seems like the crappie market is perfect for older people.

I think that we're seeing a real trend to go back to the fun of fishing and to family fishing as a unit. When you look at both of those, the thing that comes to mind first and foremost are panfish, and specifically crappie.

Many of us have the image of a father and son sitting on a dock or a riverbank with a canepole and a bobber with a worm or cricket on the hook and a number of panfish on the stringer.

11

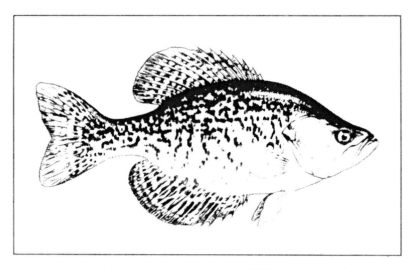

Many young fishermen get hooked on fishing in an early stage of their life and, after a few years, they "graduate" to bigger game, such as bass. They are the very same people who try to incorporate the fun of fishing back to the family; they take their kids or grandkids fishing and realize that bass may not be the ideal fish for a youngster starting to fish. They go back to the crappie for that.

Today's product trends address ultra-light tackle, spinning reels, lighter lines and even lightweight boats especially for crappie. The fish appeals to anglers of all ages. With the current emphasis on taking kids fishing, the crappie should remain a favorite fish of the masses.

Today, people are focusing more on crappie fishing as a specific fishing pursuit just as you'd fish for bass or walleye or trout. The great thing about panfishing is that it's available to everyone everywhere. In many cases, panfishing is the most fun because there's a lot of action involved with it. It's also a good way to help encourage people to get involved in fishing because it can be a very rewarding experience.

Chapter 1

LURE AND BAIT CONSIDERATIONS

Crappie fishermen usually have a good selection of artificials to consider at the tackle shop. For the angler new to the sport, such an assortment of attractive lures may confuse or over-complicate the selection process. Probably, a good way to start a selection of lures for the tackle box is to purchase one of the "Crappie Kits" that are on the shelves of many retailers.

One company has an assortment of panfish kits with lifelike replicas of bugs and other forage. The soft-molded lures are ideal for light tackle or cane pole fishing. For the beginning bait angler, one tackle box manufacturer offers a complete tackle setup, including the tackle box. The kit is a six-section swingback tray box equipped with 101 items, such as bait jar, bobbers, stringer, line clipper, split shot sinkers and other goodies.

Most lure-tossing crappie anglers will have a box full of jigs. The variety of sizes and skirt materials has never been better. For most crappie-fishing applications, a jig with a round or ball head is most appropriate. Such a lure can easily bounce off any underwater structure, and it will sink faster than most other types of heads. Bullet-shaped heads are excellent swimming heads and are effective for crappie. A productive selection of jigs for most situations should probably include skirts and plastic bodied baits. Pick up a few with adjoining spinners, and you should be ready for the pond or lake.

Some jigs have an added weight inside the head of the lure for better casting and depth penetration when after the big ones. A relatively new entry into the jig adornment market are fringe-type rubber tails that can be used on a jighead or spinner combo. They come in several popular colors.

Skirts and Colors

Jig color and skirt possibilities are endless, and most work under certain conditions. Some are tinsel-skirted for clear waters in their expansive ultralight line of productive jigs. The brilliant-colored skirts add to the attraction of jigs with small spinner blades. Color striking preferences in crappie will change from day to day and even throughout an eight-hour period. Equip the tackle box with a selection of colors, and you should have one that will entice the paper-mouth panfish.

White jigs work under most conditions, but others are also productive in the right areas. Use pink, yellow and chartreuse in clear waters, and darker hues, such as orange, purple, green, etc. in stained water. In highly vegetated waters, a green and white jig can be super productive, and in low light conditions, you may want to try a black jig.

One jig-maker offers a small jig with dots or candy stripes and a tiny 1/32 ounce spinnerbait lure for more stained waters. Crappie are always interested in jig-spinner and double-jig combos. One combo has two shad-colored dollfly heads with white or yellow maribou rigged with leaders and swivels.

Another product for beginning crappie fishermen to consider is the processed bait forms. Why not feed them the real thing? Johnson Fishing's Crappie Candy is their combination of secret ingredients in a jig tail. Uncle Josh offers feeding crappie a Panfish Pork bait. The pigskin rind features its own pork scent and has the ability to absorb other scents.

Berkley's Panfish/Crappie Power Bait is a species-specific bait that is fortified with Strike fish attractant. The bait was

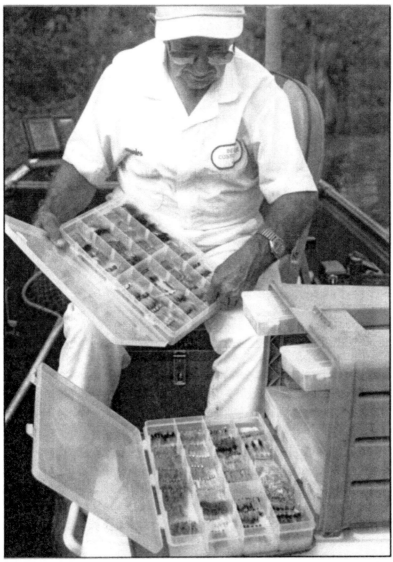

Jig color and skirt possibilities are endless, and most work under certain conditions. Some are tinsel-skirted for clear waters in their expansive ultralight line of productive jigs.

15

Favorite summertime lures evolve into smaller offerings like tiny 2-inch curl-tail grubs on leadhead jigs.

custom formulated through research in Berkley's own fish biology lab, then tested under actual fishing conditions. Results and sales of the popular bait have been exceptional. Other companies are getting into the act of processed baits, and that trend should continue.

Calendar of Events

Crappie become vulnerable to near-surface baits early in the year. While small jigs and beetle-spin type spinnerbaits are very effective, little crankbaits normally take their share of spring and fall crappie too. Favorite summertime lures start out resembling minnow-hued crankbaits and evolve into smaller offerings like tiny 2-inch curl-tail grubs on leadhead jigs during the really hot times.

Schoolers in the late summer and fall usually chase small threadfin shad around most of the lakes in the southern states.

Tail-spinner lures, shad and tiny spoons are effective for all sizes of crappie if the size correctly imitates that of the forage.

Small crankbaits in the minnow or shad colors are top crappie producers in most waters, and are most successfully fished over rock covered humps in 8 to 12 feet of water. Also toss them around the tops of submerged trees or retrieve them along underwater ridges located via a chart recorder.

The further a cool weather angler ventures from the nearest hot water source, such as a power plant discharge or natural spring or tributary, the deeper the fish will be found. Crappie can usually be caught from 15 to 25 foot depths on small jigging spoons. The larger crappie often go for jig-and-grub combinations when cold water drives them deeper to the submerged points and islands.

Silver deep-diver crankbaits trolled along a temperature breakline, that area where a thermal gradient exists, are often productive. Live minnows fished near the bottom in 20 feet of water are also excellent baits for crappie year 'round.

Whether you are tossing artificial lures or a specially-formulated bait product, you'll be wise to keep hooks sharp and formed properly. Try bending the point out ever so slightly, if you are getting strikes but not hook-ups. Use a hone or battery-operated sharpener and touch up the lure after any encounter with brush or other structure. Check the point also after any tussle with a big crappie.

17

Chapter 2

THE RIGHT EQUIPMENT

Many crappie fishermen aren't lucky enough to have guidance and assistance in selecting the right equipment. There is no need to spend a lot of money for the very best rod and reel and other gear when after America's favorite panfish. Premium equipment is something that you may wish to move up to later, once you have become relatively proficient at crappie fishing. Or, you may not.

Selecting effective rods, poles and reels without over-investing is easier today than ever before. In fact, just in the last year or two, many manufacturers have begun offering complete kits focused on the beginning angler. Most are relatively inexpensive and are appropriate for the majority of anglers interested in fishing for crappie.

Most "starter" kits are designed to get kids and families fishing together. There is no better fish than crappie for young anglers to seek, so the new emphasis from industry manufacturers is welcome. Casual, family-oriented anglers are looking for affordable and reliable products, and today they can easily get them.

Let's look briefly at rod and reel options for newcomers to the sport of crappie angling. You'll find a bewildering assortment in a tackle shop, but most crappie fishermen will be interested only in light tackle and either spinning or spincast reels. In some cases, reels aren't even necessary; a cane pole or long fiberglass pole will suffice. In fact, at many of the big, national crappie contests, many of the tournament qualifiers have their boats full of such gear. Granted, most also have conventional rods and reels and use them.

For most crappie anglers whose baits and lures are light, the equipment will consist of either spinning or spincast rods and reels. Rods have various characteristics and many today even bear specie-specific labeling, such as the graphite Buck's Crappie Rod by B'n'M Company. Not all rod companies label accordingly. Many that are appropriate for the crappie angler will be simply labeled "light-action" or "lightweight." While some anglers may prefer an ultralight outfit, the standard rod fare should have good backbone and a light tip action.

Length is a matter of personal preference. Long rods are awkward to some and the very short 2' rods may be suitable for children only. Most beginners will find a 5' to 5 1/2' fiberglass rod with some flexibility to be sufficient and appropriate. When buying a rod separate from the reel, be sure to get the same type of rod. For example, a spinning reel that normally hangs under the rod would require a straight-handled spinning rod which has large guides for the line that loops off of the reel. Correspondingly, a spin cast reel would be matched with a rod that has smaller guides and either a straight or pistol-grip handle.

With a little casting practice, open face spinning reels are relatively easy to use. With a balanced rod and reel and properly spooled line, beginners will have little problem becoming proficient. Spinning gear is slightly more sensitive to a light strike, but twisted and loose line can occasionally occur, and that will frustrate beginners (and some experts).

Closed-Face Equipment and Kits

By far the easiest reel to master is the closed-face spincast. It is the one that most everyone starts out with, and one that many anglers keep using. I can remember graduating from my cane poles to the Johnson Century and Citation some 35 years ago

By far the easiest reel to master is the closed-face spincast. It is the one that most everyone starts out with, and one that many anglers keep using.

when I was a kid. The spincast reels of today are much improved than the earlier versions, of course. They are more durable and have less line tangles.

Most crappie fishermen will find spincast equipment to be the most economical. The push button line release is very easy to master, and it will handle the light lures that spinning gear will. Casting accuracy and distance may be slightly less, but for most situations, that won't matter.

"Most casting problems begin to occur when fishermen put on a line that is lighter or heavier than the spool diameter can accommodate," explains Ron Sundborg, Director of Marketing

A bucket full of minnows and the right equipment is all you need to enjoy crappie fishing.

for Johnson. "If the line is too light, it can fly off in tangled loops; if it's too heavy, it often comes off like a coiled spring."

As a result, many manufacturers are now offering kits or combos with the proper line already on a specific reel. Some companies offer several models of long-cast, "trouble-free" Crappie outfits. The majority of combos have reels spooled with 6 to 8 pound test line and a graphite composite light action rod between 5 and 6 feet long. Many companies offer pre-packaged spinning and spincast fishing combos that come with monofilament. The ready-to-fish kits often include a two-piece rod with reel, plus a selection of terminal tackle as well.

One manufacturer even offers an inexpensive 91-piece spincast fishing outfit that includes a two-piece 5' rod, spincast reel, line, live bait fishing necessities and a few lures. Many

When you set the hook on crappie, easy does it. The "slab" will grab a jig and slowly swim off.

companies today have also targeted youngsters under the age of 10 with their character series of ready-to-fish rod and reel combos.

Ultralight and Flyfishing Fun

You don't need a stiff rod to set the hook on these fish and an ultralight is really the way to go on them. Several companies manufacture miniature rod and reels that can put a lot of fun into your life and food on the table at the same time. Pick a quality outfit though for longevity.

A light action rod is especially critical for the tender mouth fish. When you set the hook on crappie, easy does it. The "slab" will grab a jig and slowly swim off. When you notice the line move, gently but firmly lift the pole upward. If you set the hook into a snag, the hook will usually straighten out, provided the line you're using is strong enough. When you retrieve the hook simply bend the thin wire hook back into the original shape with a pair of long-nosed pliers.

23

Although the long pole and ultralight spinning outfits lend themselves well to crappie fishing, a light fly rod can also provide great fun. Fly rod addicts often spend much of their speck fishing hours with the light wand in their hands. Popular fly rod artificials are fly rod spoons, fly and spinner combinations and streamer flies.

In flyfishing for crappie, a slow but active retrieve is usually a must. Let the lure sink nearly to the bottom, then retrieve with erratic jerks pausing for several seconds between each jerk.

To find the right equipment, it is best to visit your local tackle store and try out the gear. The salesman can help you match the rod, reel and line, or you may want to go with one of the great inexpensive combo outfits that hang on the walls.

Chapter 3

STRIKE DETECTION - HOOKS AND BOBBERS

Newcomers to bait fishing for crappie often employ light line but then add things like a huge cork and thick shank hook. For this paper-mouthed panfish, that's overkill, and the use of such will hurt productivity, rather than help it. As with any species, balanced tackle right down to the terminal tackle is vital to success.

Walk into any tackle shop and ask for a hook and bobber, and you'll find shelves and racks full of the various models made for a variety of species and uses. There are literally thousands of hook types and sizes, all designed for specific needs of anglers. Material varies, as does the coloration. Many opt for gold or chrome which may offer an additional attraction to the bait. Other expert crappie anglers will leave the silver-plated hooks on the shelf and selected a cadmium or dark-painted finish for minimum visibility.

When the crappie move into cover, live bait still fishing is a good method to try. The fish can usually be found in shallow water (4 to 8 feet) during the spring spawn and often require the fisherman to thread his way inside some heavy cover. No more than a long pole, small bobber, split shot, sharp hook and live minnows are needed. In fact, this rig is highly recommended.

A few basic tackle principles should be incorporated for a deadly rig. A small, sharp hook of thin wire will allow the minnow to show considerably more life than would on a larger, heavier hook. A fine wire, long-shanked Aberdeen hook is, in fact, ideal for most crappie fishing. Size it according to the size of minnow being used: No. 4 for the small to medium size baitfish and No. 2 for large Missouri minnows when after the trophy size "specks." Too large a hook can keep crappie from striking, or worse yet, tear through its mouth when it does bite.

The fine wire hook penetrates a minnow with a minimum of damage to its liveliness, and can be easily straightened while being pulled from a snag. It is easy to reshape the hook and continue fishing without having to spend time re-rigging. Like any type of fishing, sharp points and barbs are important, even on the smaller, thinner-diameter hooks.

One way to hook a minnow for crappie is through the forward part of the eye sockets. With a light wire hook this can be done without actually piercing the eyeball, and the skull bones of the minnow serve as reinforcement against the hook tearing out. Minnows also can be hooked through both lips, and back or just forward of the tail. But take care not to pierce the backbone or the bait won't live very long.

Floats, Bobbers & Corks

The fun part of using a float or bobber is watching it. The slightest tremblings builds anticipation that the quarry is near. The minnow may be getting nervous or excited. The suspense builds until the bobber bobs or disappears. Then, the excitement intensifies and you battle the fish to the boat or shore.

Floats come in a variety of shapes. Some that are ideal for casting are pointed on one end and have are wide at the other. Its buoyancy can be adjusted by adding water to a built-in reservoir. Another pencil-shaped float is also ideal for long casts. A bead or plastic float stop is needed to rig the bobber. A stop knot can also be tied up the line at the point where you want the float to be positioned above the bait. While those are slip floats, stick floats are also popular with more experienced crappie fishermen.

The fun part of using a float or bobber is watching it. The slightest tremblings builds anticipation that the quarry is near. The minnow may be getting nervous or excited. The suspense builds until the bobber bobs or disappears.

Possibly the easiest to use are the small, round red and white bobbers with a tiny wire loop at each end. You just clamp your line into the loops at the appropriate point above your bait or jig. The stream-lined corks may be the best, however, because they can often be pulled under and even through the water with minimal resistance. That's best to prevent the crappie from detecting the unnatural object holding back its supper.

Prime Rigging

When fishing in two feet of water, for example, a small bobber about 1 1/2 foot above the jig will suspend it off the

When fishing in two feet of water, a small bobber about 1 1/2 foot above the jig will help suspend it off the bottom. The bobber will bounce at the slightest strike, making for easy detection.

bottom. The bobber will bounce at the slightest strike making for easy detection. The bobber shouldn't be too buoyant, or it might arouse the suspicions of light-biting crappies and cause them to drop the bait before you can hook them. A quill float is best, but a small, slender cork is also satisfactory.

The effectiveness of any float rig depends on the buoyancy and size of bobber, the weight (lead and/or minnow) hanging from it and the length of line between them. With some active minnows, you'll only need a split shot or two, assuming that the float is sized correctly. Too much weight may sink the float or inhibit the minnow's action. In some cases you may not wish to use additional weight; let the minnow roam around on its own while in relatively shallow water.

When you are not sure about the depth of the crappie, set out several rigs (check your state regulations of limit) and place the floats at different depths. Once a fish is caught, then place all baits at that depth by adjusting the other floats. Keep a couple of feet of line between the bobber and hook if possible, and you'll find some action!

Chapter 4

UNTANGLING LINE MESS

Line options can be confusing, even to those anglers with a great deal of experience. A newcomer to the sport may not be able to obtain appropriate information about quality and applications differences. Tackle considerations and fishing methods vary, and so should the selection of line.

The weakest link in terminal tackle is usually the line. It can be damaged simply by use, or through other means such as UV exposure from the sun's rays. Line is the most important component of the crappie angler's tackle. A good quality monofilament is usually satisfactory for most fishing conditions.

Popular lines today also include copolymers, multi-polymers, alloys and braids. Some specially-formulated lines resist UV and ozone deterioration and others solve specific cold and solar problems. For the beginner, though, the line considerations are less high-tech. Forget the marketing buzz words and buy a quality line based on the following general considerations.

Abrasion resistance is important whether you are wrapping the line repeated around a cane pole or casting and retrieving over vegetation or brush. Stretch is not generally a factor for ''paper-mouth'' crappie. You don't need to generate a strike shock to set the hook on this fish. Most of the fishing will be relatively close to you.

Diameter is a line characteristic that should be considered. While you don't have to search out the very thinnest in the world,

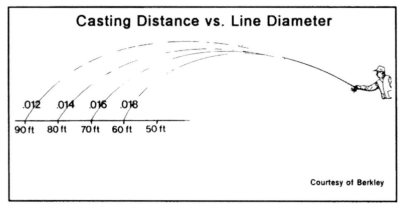

Casting Distance vs. Line Diameter

.012   .014   .016   .018

90 ft   80 ft   70 ft   60 ft   50 ft

Courtesy of Berkley

most good quality lines will be engineered for minimum line diameter. There is always a trade-off as to what pound test line you will use for smallest diameter and maximum strength.

It is wise to let the conditions and tackle dictate the line size. For example, a cane pole user may employ 4 to 6 pound test line

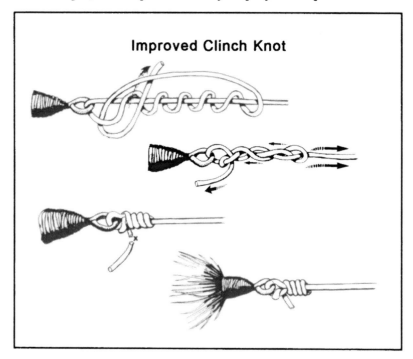

Improved Clinch Knot

Palomar Knot

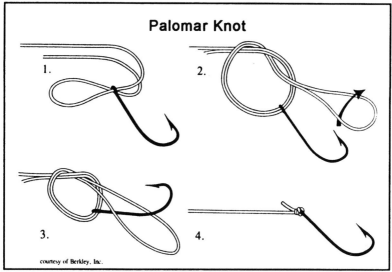

courtesy of Berkley, Inc.

in open water drifting and 8 to 10 in shallow vegetation. An angler using spinning gear may use from 4 to 8 pound line with those conditions, while a spincaster might find 6 to 10 pound test the most appropriate line for the reel and rod.

Filling a Spinning Reel

Affix the reel to the rod and string the line through the guides. Flip open the bail and knot the line tightly to the spool. Flip the bail closed. Have another person hold the supply spool so the line spirals off the supply spool in the same coil direction as you want it to go onto the reel spool. Tension the line using the thumb and index finger of your rod-holding hand. Fill spinning-reel spools to slightly below the spool lip.

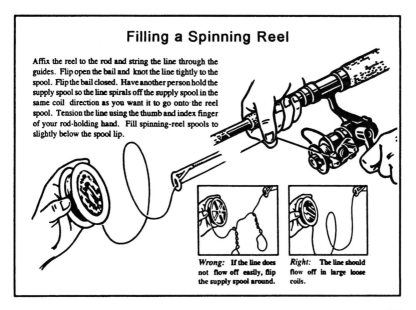

Wrong: If the line does not flow off easily, flip the supply spool around.

Right: The line should flow off in large loose coils.

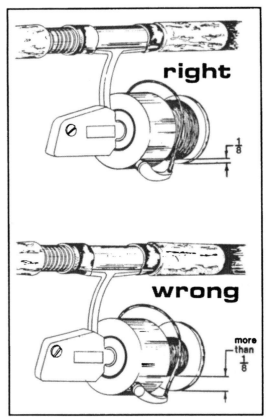

The correct way to put line on a spinning reel spool is to fill it to slightly below the lip.

Spool memory is denoted by the coils of line that sometimes take a "set" on reels. While not as offensive on spinning and spincast reels, coils slow down casting effectiveness and increase backlashes, so they should be avoided. Do that by making sure the line you buy is "limp" or has low spool memory. Fortunately, most quality lines are relatively limp.

Visibility and Strength

Crappie strikes are often soft, and line watchers appreciate a line that is highly visible above water and less visible beneath the surface. Photochromic and fluorescent lines are best to detect strikes when not relying on a bobber, especially in shaded or deeper waters and around cover.

Filling a Closed-Face Spincast Reel

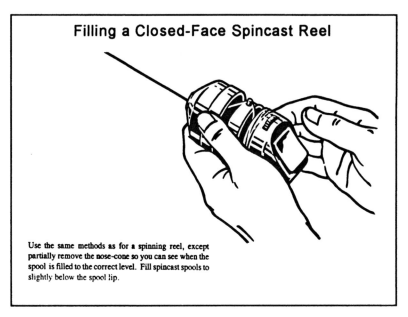

Use the same methods as for a spinning reel, except partially remove the nose-cone so you can see when the spool is filled to the correct level. Fill spincast spools to slightly below the spool lip.

Tensile strength and knot strength are the final two considerations that are important. Both are vital to landing a large crappie or other sizable fish on any gear. Those are two characteristics that are controllable in manufacturing, and as long as you protect the line from excessive heat, prolonged sunlight and chemicals, it should retain its strength.

When you spool on the line, follow the instructions on the fresh spool or in the line box. For spinning reels, string the line through the first couple of guides, open the bait and knot the line to the spool. Holding the outfit several feet away from the supply spool, keep tension on the line with the thumb and forefinger and reel the line on the spool. Make sure that the line is spiraling off the supply spool in the same coil direction that it is going onto the reel. The line will develop twists if you don't pay attention to that factor. Fill spool to slightly below the lip.

With spincast reels, it is best to loosen the nose cone and hold it in front of the spool when filling. That will allow you to see how full the spool has become. Fill it to slightly below the lip

An angler using spinning gear may use from 4 to 8 pound line with those varying conditions, while a spincaster might find 6 to 10 pound test the most appropriate line for the reel and rod.

also. Check for abraded line and unwanted knots during you fishing trip. Look at the first three feet from the hook after each strike or fish. Check line level after any on-the-water breakage and replace when that level is low enough to inhibit casting. Be sure and throw the old, abraded line into the trash barrel at home, or recycle it at your local tackle shop.

As a minimum, replace line once a year. You'll minimize potential problems that way. If you fish several days each week, quicker replacement may be necessary. Better yet, once you have landed a few hundred crappie, replace it then!

Chapter 5

SPAWNING SLABS

It isn't easy to pick up a rod and reel for the first time in nine months and go catch 100 crappie in three short hours. And, semester tests for five college courses coming up within four days doesn't help a student's concentration. It was final exam week at the university, but there was no way I was going to miss the fantastic crappie action at the nearby reservoir.

Numerous reports of great catches of "slabs" were coming from Turtle Creek Reservoir in northern Kansas each day. I was attending Kansas State University at the time. Fortunately, it was only six miles from the lake, which allowed me several days of action that all of us should have several times in our lives.

The warm May days had increased my fishing fever to a point where I just had to put the books aside and pick up my fishing rod. I was young and foolish (maybe not so) then; it was time for a change of pace. I was joined that weekend by my parents and younger brother, who were also looking forward to the holiday and to verify the good fishing reports.

The weather was windy and overcast when we arrived at the lake. We rented a small aluminum boat at the marina and strapped our 10-horsepower outboard on it. The four of us headed out into the whitecaps with really no idea as to where we might locate the bevy of crappie we had heard about. Most of the coves were covered with flooded timber, and they all looked similar.

About half-way across the lake, we realized that we had misjudged the wind intensity. Fortunately, at least then, the wind was blowing in the direction we wished to go. We passed up two small coves with a few submerged trees in each, and ducked into one with several hundred flooded trees that were spread over the entire cove. Once inside the cove and out of the wind, we noticed two other boats moored in the trees near the mouth. They were fishing with live minnows and bobbers.

We worked our small boat into the submerged trees and anchored in about four feet of water. My parents flipped out minnows while my brother Ron and I cast small marabou jigs in and around the heavy brush. After one hour we had received very little action from the crappie, so we moved deeper into the cove. My father and mother stayed with their two-inch minnows which, with the aid of a float, were fished just off the bottom.

Shallow Bedding

In the cove, the water clarity of about 18 inches varied little as we moved further toward the back using the small electric motor to propel our craft. We managed to work our way through the tangled trees and stopped in an area with a depth of two feet. The water seemed too shallow, but just as soon as my jig hit the water, I had a nice one-pound crappie smack it. My brother followed suit and momentarily, my parents each also caught a nice fat crappie.

Short 8- to 10-foot casts became shorter and shorter since we were taking a fish each cast. They were mostly the dark black males, but occasionally a belly-bulging female would come on board. We soon realized that all we had to do to take all we wanted was to drop a jig over the side and jig it up and down once or twice.

We each caught several big crappie, some up to 2 1/2 pounds. Those are big crappie on any lake anywhere. The average weight of our crappie was about 1 1/4 pounds, which is one of the best "average weights" of panfish that I've seen, before or since.

Crappie are usually residents of deep-water structure, yet they can be caught in scant inches when they're planning their spawning festivities.

As we moved slowly through the flooded trees, we took crappie each time that we dropped a jig next to a tree trunk. The depth was generally one to two feet, but we found the crappie even shallower. My parents soon ran out of minnows and turned to jigs, which were more productive anyway. Baiting up was taking them twice as long as catching the fat slabs. The jigs were just a lot more efficient.

The action never stopped. We finished the day having caught around 150, of which we kept too many, not because we surpassed our limit, we didn't, but because we had to clean them. That was my first experience with spawning crappie more years ago than I care to remember.

While crappie are usually residents of deep-water structure, there are times when they can be caught in scant inches, generally when they're planning their spawning festivities. They are early spawners and can be found in that ''condition'' from December to April, depending on the region where you live. Crappie in the South may become very active as early as Christmas. During spawning times, they are the easiest to catch of the entire sunfish family, if you can locate them.

Millions of crappie move out of the open lake and into rivers, creeks, canals, coves and near shorelines during spawning runs. When the spawning urge arrives, males move into the shallower areas and start to set up home in the grass and around the bulrushes. Egg-laden females can then normally be taken in open stretches at depths of 12 to 15 feet.

Spawning activity may be initiated by a cold front in the southern regions of the country and by photoperiod (period of daylight) and pH values of the water. Dark males will take off for the shallows initially and start fanning beds. The right conditions may occur from December to April or even May, depending on where in the country you live. In most states, the first full moon in February or March will cause the female crappie to move into the shallows and start actual egg laying.

Spawning Behavior

Like the largemouth bass, the male searches out clean sand or sand-gravel bottoms in the shallows and prepares the spawning bed by fanning away debris. Then, as weather conditions become right, the females cluster over the beds and lay millions of eggs. Once the females reach the spawning beds and congregate, catches improve and everyone takes crappie.

Shallow spawning activity will normally continue for several weeks and maintain a fast pace. On one memorable day back also when I was trying to balance good grades in college with my interest in fishing, spawning crappie got me into some trouble. The reservoir near the campus was producing great crappie fishing, so two of my college buddies and I took off for the lake at 4 p.m. to spend a couple of hours with the crappie.

We decided to have a fishing contest that afternoon. Not that catching 67 to my two friend's 65 and 53 in about three hours really proved that much. It was really a matter only of who was

38

Fishing with minnows is a common means to catch a 'boatload' of spawning crappie.

the quickest. The following days' contests were very similar in results, but on one occasion, one of my fishing buddies wanted a few to eat.

The student had a place to keep them frozen - his fraternity house, but he claimed they wouldn't let him clean them there. So, we decided to keep a dozen or so of the 150 plus we took that day and stopped at the dormitory where I lived to clean the fish. The dorm, located under a football stadium, had a huge washroom and shower area which I thought would be an ideal place.

My ''dorm Mother'' had a different idea, though, particularly when she saw my buddy's fraternity sweat shirt. She thought initially that we were both from outside the dorm and were simply using the washroom to clean the fish. Even after clearing up that misconception, she was very upset at us for clogging up two of the 15 wash basins with scales and entrails. Needless to say, we had a job for a couple of hours cleaning up that facility.

39

Wooded coves are often excellent places to find spawning crappie. The pH value in submerged timber is often ideal and the protection factor of a dense forest in extremely shallow water is difficult to top. Coves that offer slowly tapering bottoms with wood habitat are preferred by spawning crappie. The limited access to adjacent deep water prevents an ''influx'' of predators from the depths. Largemouth bass, for example, normally hunt for their forage near deep-water access.

Fingerling Prey

Larger crappie seldom need to fear a bass unless the predator is four or five times the size. Fingerling specks do. They are preyed upon by most every fish that swims in fresh waters.

The fact that crappie spawn ahead of the bass population may also be significant. They get first shot at some of the nice sandy bed areas, but the down side of that is that their fry are the first foraging ''targets'' each spring.

When the crappie are on their beds, they are susceptible to most small lures and live baits. I've caught several on plugs as large as Norman's Little ''N''. They'll hit whatever they can get their mouth around. At times, larger crappie will go after a slow-crawling plastic worm. The one thing that I've noticed, though, is that the slower the bait is worked, the more strikes it will produce. A jig that is dropped near their bed and slowly ''swims'' around should draw a strike almost immediately.

Often, it's just a matter of introducing the lure into the area. A slowly-moving spinnerbait or grub will attract the fish's attention quickly. Naturally, live Missouri minnows or freshly-caught grass shrimp will draw the quick response, but it just takes longer to present that bait to the fish.

Fishing with minnows is a common means to catch a 'boatload' of spawning crappie. Small minnows between one and two inches are normally hooked through both eye sockets with a fine wire hook when trolling relatively shallow water. A few split shot six inches above the hook will keep the minnow at a specific depth. Most anglers try to keep their baits off the bottom, a foot

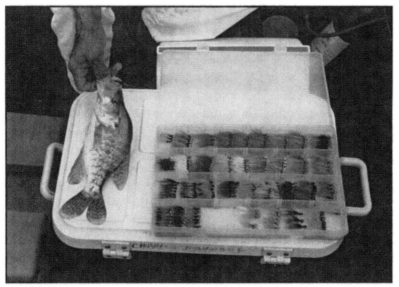

Productive anglers carry along several 1/8 ounce jigs in a variety of colors for those times when the crappie are discerning. On some days, only one exact combination will suit them, and you might wear yourself out trying to convince them otherwise.

or so. A small float helps to detect strikes on 'unattended' poles or rods. One that has very little resistance is best.

Jig-minnow combinations also are successful on huge schools of crappie that seem to bite day and night during the spawning season. Small spinners, plastic grubs, and streamers are effective lures at times, but many believe that the jig is probably the deadliest spring bait ever. A marabou jig has more action than one tied with hair or hackles. It will pulse, quiver, and wiggle at the slightest rod tip movement.

Productive anglers carry along several 1/8 ounce jigs in a variety of colors for those times when the crappie are discerning. On some days, only one exact combination will suit them, and you might wear yourself out trying to convince them otherwise.

If the wind is up, drifting without using an electric motor can be productive. Otherwise, some motion should be imparted to

41

the jig. Smart anglers will vary the movement and color schemes offered until they find the right combination. Trollers often find that little jig motion is needed when the boat provides propulsion.

Tackle For The Spawn

Light line is preferred by most crappie jiggers, since it allows the lure to move naturally. Line thickness won't scare off the soft-mouthed panfish either. Ultra light spinning tackle and line sizes of between four and six pound test is ideal for this action. Even the basic cane pole can be employed.

Two jigs can be placed three feet apart for maximum coverage. The distance between the lures will also help determine the level of the spawning crappie, once one has been fooled. When you have two takers, you may also find that the larger fish will be affixed to the lower hook. The preferred jig colors on many spring waters are yellow and white, or combinations of the two, but at times other hues work well.

A tandem hook rig can be used by minnow users too, but that's sometimes dangerous. Two large specks on a light rig can mount a formidable battle. That's not uncommon in the spring during spawning season. Since crappie won't do a lot of chasing after baits in colder waters, speed control and bait placement is important. When a lure or bait is near, however, several from the school may want it.

Crappie in a pre-spawn situation tend to "ball up" at a level where pH, oxygen, and temperature are suitable. Larger specimens are often near the bottom of the group and placing the bait deeper will give you a better chance at a king-sized fish.

Night angling around concrete structures with bug-attracting lanterns is also productive during the spawn. Minnows will feed on the insects, and the hungry crappie won't be far behind.

Shallow water crappie are worth searching for and finding in the spring. They will provide more action then in a short period than at any other time of year. Try the shallows this spring!

Chapter 6

HOT WEATHER OPPORTUNITIES

"How about a change of pace?" asked my friend as he dropped our fourth largemouth into the live well.

"Sounds good to me," I said. "We may get very wet in a few minutes anyway."

He moved the boat further into the treeline and reached for his seven and a half foot crappie pole. The light spinning outfit was pre-rigged with a small jig for just such an occasion: slow bass fishing. Our four hours of bass chasing in the dead calm with 95-degree heat had left us drenched from perspiration.

Rain clouds were threatening, however, and finally a cool wind 'shift' occurred as I pulled up my first crappie, a fat two pounder. The temperature must have plummeted to the low 80's in just a minute or two and quickly put a freeze on us. But the crappie did not become frigid and continued to hit our small yellow maribou jigs.

The boat was nosed into the small 'cuts' that were formed in the tree-bound water hyacinths. And, more often than not, we pulled a nice sized crappie out from the stuff. The water depth was eight to ten feet beneath the hyacinths, but most of our action came from the five feet strata.

The long rod was very effective due to it reaching near the hyacinth line at all times and even reaching to pockets or holes

43

back in the stuff. The jigging motion generally was effective for the fish and, at times, several crappie were taken from the same spot.

The wind blew hard, pelting us with rain droplets for about an hour, but our protected location back in the flooded trees prevented any difficulties controlling the boat. The slower moving pace of 'speck' fishing allowed us to stay drier in the pounding rain and the action made the period of 'typhoon' onslaught pass much quicker.

The hour break was indeed interesting and my partner and I had over 30 nice crappie crowded into the boat's live well. They ranged from one to two pounds and provided the necessary meat for a planned Sunday noon fish fry the following day. The fast action gave us enthusiasm for the quarry.

Crappie have never been known as great fighters, although a two pounder will definitely put up a fight, but they're without a doubt a lot of fun to catch. When the fish have been located, it is easy to catch a bunch. Finding a limit in the summer heat, though, can sometimes be very challenging.

Crappie have a paper-thin mouth and the tackle must be delicate to prevent tearouts. That isn't made simpler, either, by the proximity to brush, aquatic plants, or logs. When you do hook one and get him near the boat, a net will increase your chances of having him for supper.

Bait Movement

In heavy cover, it is best to relocate your bait frequently. If one small pothole doesn't produce a strike, the bait should be picked up and placed in another. Also with a long pole, the catch is more easily hoisted out of the dense cover. Once the crappie have moved shallow, thousands of 'speck' anglers can join them.

The crappie can withstand heavy fishing pressure. Catching several of them by everyone has little effect on their species, as denoted by typically high bag limits set on crappie. They are prolific enough to maintain their numbers and, if they are not

During the summer months, crappie generally hang around fallen trees, bridges, lily pads, hyacinths and other cover in four feet or more of water.

fished for often enough, they can overpopulate some bodies of water.

A small lake or pond may contain several nice size crappie. Unless fishing pressure is quite heavy in such places, the chances are better then ever that the crappie will be stunted in growth. When they overpopulate small bodies of water, the average size is very small. But their numbers can remain quite high.

Most of the better hot-weather lakes for "specks" are usually the deeper ones. A common feature in the better lakes is depths of at least 15 feet. For the females in deep water, most anglers prefer to drift with the wind using weighted tandem-hook rigs baited with small minnows fished on the bottom. This popular technique is used extensively and many anglers are equipped with three rods and reels, plus rigs featuring as many hooks.

During the summer months, crappie generally hang around fallen trees, bridges, lily pads, hyacinths and other cover in four feet or more of water. In creeks, give attention to bends where the banks are cut deep and to the mouths of branch streams and coves.

45

TWO DOZEN TOP FLORIDA CRAPPIE WATERS	
WATER	**REGION**
Crescent Lake	Northeast
Lake Dexter	
Lake George	
Salt Springs Run	
Blue Cypress Lake	East Central
Lake Kissimmee	
Lake Marian	
Lake Monroe	
Lake Poinsett	
Middle River (St. Johns)	
St. Johns (Astor)	
West Lake Tohopekaliga	
Lake Okeechobee	South
Lake Trafford	
Lake Griffin	West Central
Lake Hancock	
Lake Harris	
Lake Hatchineha	
Lake Rousseau	
Lake Thonotosassa	
Winter Haven Chain	
Lake Lochloosa	Northwest
Newnans Lake	
Orange Lake	

You'll often find crappie on or over deep shady structure where the water temperature is cool and the water highly oxygenated. Actually they will often suspend at one specific depth level and not move far from it.

Depth Du Jour

It is then very important to determine their depth on a given day and keep your bait in that zone. Since crappie do suspend, locating the right depth is the key to filling a stringer.

The crappie can be located by checking out several depths at one time until the most productive is found. At that time, most crappie addicts like the ease and quickness of a jig to catch several. Good artificial lure fishermen often prefer a white or yellow-colored jig.

Many lunker fishermen use a 1/4 ounce size while others like the smaller 1/8 or 1/16 ounce jigs. It is sometimes best to start with the larger and go progressively smaller until you're able to determine the size of baitfish the crappie are interested in. Such is extremely importantly. In fact, many of the theories, facts and analysis techniques in my first book, "Follow The Forage For Better Bass Angling" hold true for the crappie. That book on predator/prey relationships is available for $11.95 (includes postage and handling charges). Check out the order information in the Resource Directory at the back of this book.

Jigs that closely imitate the forage are very versatile. There are several ways a jig can be worked, and actually, it is very hard to retrieve this lure incorrectly. Any movement of the marabou jig imparts a breathing, life-like action to the lure.

Most experts prefer the feathered jig, with marabou being the favorite. The lightweight feathers respond to any twitching or jigging action imparted by the rod tip. The best summer crappie retrieve on most Florida waters is the slow twitch, but you should vary the retrieve if that fails.

Crappie jigs should have a small sharp wire hook which is gold plated. The purpose here is to have a bendable, thin wire hook so that we are able to pull out of snags without losing the lure and re-bend the wire into shape. This thin, sharp hook is easier to "set" lightly into the crappie's paper mouth.

Hot Weather Structure

A top spot to look for crappie is around piers, floating docks and bridge abutments. With your depth located, find the submerged riverbed in man-made impoundments, and if the river bend is within reachable depth, fish the deep holes in the bends which have brush in them.

If you fish the shallow natural lakes and there is no deep water, fish the heaviest cover or weedbeds you can find during summertime.

Shallow brush piles, weed beds and clumps of grass should be fished in the spring. When you deplete an area (noticed by the action slowing down) move on to faster action. As with other game fish, the depth they will be at is determined greatly by water clarity and sunlight conditions.

Fish deeper on a bright day and shallower on a dark or overcast day, or at night. If a cool front comes through during the late spring, fish deeper. If the crappie were at two feet before the cold front, they have probably put aside their spawning activities and moved.

If you can't locate them in the shoreline cover, around docks or bridge abutments, and under permanently anchored boats then trolling can be tried. A good means to find them is by drifting or trolling at different depth levels in open water.

Many explore various depths by slow trolling with small jigs, spinner baits or minnows. It is really just a matter of preference.

Regardless of the bait or method used, the crappie is to many anglers a unique and interesting change of pace. He's not an explosive, acrobatic fish not a powerful, surging bruiser. No, the respectable crappie is not even a bass at all. Nor does he have to be.

Chapter 7

RELEASE YOUR TROPHY CATCH?

Once you've hooked that giant crappie that you've been tossing lures or Missouri minnows at all day long, what then? If he's a prize catch, should you mount him or release him (after a few photos) to provide more thrills yet for another angler or even you again!

Most crappie fishermen in this day and age are concerned about the future of the species, regardless of how prolific they may seem. We were told in the past that the species can easily over-populate small bodies of water and that we should keep most of the crappie that we catch. But, is that always a wise choice for a trophy?

Today, many anglers keep only those fish that they wish to mount or put on their table. A mess of freshly caught ''specks'' can definitely provide a feast, and the species is a survivor. But piling them up in the freezer to await freezer burn is a waste of a valuable natural resource. Why not just release the biggest?

The key to releasing a large crappie is to handle it as little as possible. If an angler wants to return the fish to the water, then he should carefully release it immediately after landing it.

If the sportsman wants to play the fish out by battling it for a while, he may overstress the fish and making it much more susceptible to infections and predators. If the crappie is played out to a 'belly-up' condition, it is probably in shock and lacks oxygen, and the chances of its survival are minimal.

The best way to release the fish is to leave it in the water and back the hook out with long-nose pliers, if possible. If this isn't feasible, don't just flip the "speck" into the bottom of the boat to flop around. A bouncing fish may rupture internal organs or break the protective slime coating that its body carries.

A net should never be used if you are planning on returning the fish to the water. A fish thrashing in a knotted net mesh will damage his own slime coating and possibly tear out scales. If you release a fish that has spent several minutes in a net, it will probably develop an infection and die slowly.

Wet Hands, Happy Fish

If a net must be used, leave it partly submerged while you unhook the fish. If you must handle the fish to remove the hook, wet your hands first.

Handling the fish with dry hands can scrape off some of the protective slime coating and make a fungus infection probable, eventually causing the fish's death. Without the slime protection, the skin beneath the scales is susceptible to a variety of bacteria that can kill the crappie within two or three weeks.

Be careful of gripping the fish too tightly around its mid section. Chances of damaging their internal organs by squeezing too hard are high if too much pressure is used on a wiggling, slippery fish.

Sticking your fingers through their gills is not a good idea either, since this method will likely damage the ability of the fish to convert oxygen from the water passing through its gills, causing certain death. Keep your fingers out from under the gill flaps, and if any blood at all is present on the crappie do not return it to the water. It will likely not survive the injury.

Crappie are not known for their "bite". Their teeth are less pronounced than most other species. A large specimen can easily be gripped by the lower jaw. Insert your thumb into their mouth and lift up. This position will allow you to quickly remove the

Great care should be used in handling a crappie of any size that is going to be released. Anglers kill many fish each year that they 'throw back to grow' only through improper handling techniques.

hook and snap a picture without having to handle the rest of his body before releasing it.

Letting the crappie bang around in the bottom of the boat, in a bucket, in a wire net or dragging him up a bank can decrease its chance of survival, since the protective slime is easily damaged. Likewise, dragging the fish around on a stringer for even a few hours is dangerous to the health of the fish. Don't wait to release it.

Proper Confinement

There is always a danger in trying to keep a fish alive for any length of time in warmer surface water when it was caught from a deeper, cooler area. A livewell is always your best bet. A well-aerated livewell is now a standard item in many boats, and is necessary to keep the fish cool and healthy.

My boat is equipped with a dual livewell aeration system which includes an automatic timer. That allows me to aerate one

51

or both wells for a minute and then it will shut off for two before recycling. It is a super system, and one I wouldn't be without. I've found a livewell without an aerator in the hot summer months to be essentially useless for keeping crappie alive.

Even a deep-hooked fish has a chance of survival if the hook is removed carefully with fisherman's pliers or disgorgers. Do not tear the hook out or use grips or clams around its mid-section. If the hook is too deep to take out, leave it in. To make sure it won't block food passage you can clip the line near the hook. The digestive juices will eventually dissolve the hook.

Although the colder the water temperature, the better a fish's chance of survival will be, if the hook is removed properly the crappie will probably survive even in the summer time.

Great care should be used in handling a crappie of any size that is going to be released. Anglers kill many fish each year that they 'throw back to grow' only through improper handling techniques. Keeping the fish out for a long period of time (for photos, for instance) without submerging it in the water every few moments will not help the stressful situation.

Once you are ready to release the fish, grasp it by the lower jaw if the mouth is large enough or over the top of its head. Then, slowly swim the crappie in a ''figure eight'' to make water flow through its gills (but not backwards!).

You should be able to tell when the fish has regained its strength. To aid the future of our fisheries, we must try to release properly all crappie that we do not intend to eat or mount.

Chapter 8

MOUNT YOUR TROPHY CATCH

A true trophy fish can be mounted to provide many a memory for years, if a photograph is not sufficient. But, whether the successful angler wishes to mount or release the fish, great care is needed in its handling. Once you have caught your once-in-a-lifetime fish and can't bear to release it, proper handling is important for it to reach the den wall as the beautiful trophy you remember.

To preserve one of the great moments in your life, certain precautions should be taken prior to getting it to the taxidermist. The first thing you should do when you land the lunker is take several good quality color photos of the freshly caught crappie so that a taxidermist can reproduce the exact coloration in his studio. Once a fish is out of his environment for any length of time, it will lose some of its natural color.

The coloration of a fish can vary from one area of a lake to another depending on water clarity, vegetation and algae and bottom soil-type, so this photo is important.

Handle the trophy with great care and protect it from damage to the body, scales and fins. Don't allow it to bang around in the boat or wire net for any length of time. Rough treatment is hard to repair in the taxidermy shop.

Keep the crappie moist and take it to the taxidermist as soon as possible after the catch. Do not put it on a stringer and drag it all over the lake through weed beds, submerged brush, etc., which can mar your trophy.

If an aerated livewell is part of the equipment in your boat, put the fish in there for the transfer to the taxidermist. But, if the fish can't tolerate the warm surface waters and dies, put it on ice immediately. It will start to decompose if left in water or a warm place.

The crappie can remain on ice for up to two days. If the trophy will not reach the taxidermist in that time, then freeze it to maintain the quality. Don't attempt to skin out the fish by yourself; leave that job to the taxidermist. You will probably only ruin the condition of the fish if you lay a knife on it.

Pre-Freeze Care

Before you freeze it, a few precautions should be taken. Since the fins are very brittle upon freezing, they should be protected. A folded piece of cardboard can be placed over the tail and secured with paper clips to keep it flat and protected.

The other fins should be tight against the body before the fish is wrapped in wet cloth. The wrapped fish should then be put in a plastic lawn bag and rubber bands should be used to keep it air tight. Then, wrap it in freezer paper and tape it shut.

Don't attempt to use newspaper for the initial wrap as they both dry the fish out by absorbing the body's moisture and "bleed" on the fish as it thaws out. Newspaper is also hard to get off the fish.

The wrapped crappie should be laid flat in the freezer and frozen in that position. Nothing should be placed on top of it either while it is freezing or after it is frozen solid, since damage could result.

Freezing the trophy with the innards intact will not harm the quality of the meat, and the taxidermist may be able to save it for you. A fish that is frozen hard can be shipped by air or bus to the taxidermist of your choice. The fish should be wrapped with

54

Call the taxidermist to let him know that the fish is coming and how you want it mounted. Include a letter with specific instructions on the mount and the photo of the freshly-caught trophy.

several more layers of paper and boxed in a carton full of a good insulator such as plastic bubble sheets.

Be sure to call the taxidermist and let him know that the fish is coming and tell him how you want it mounted. Follow this up with a letter giving him specific instructions on the mount and include the photo of the freshly-caught trophy.

Fiberglass Mounts

Many taxidermists recommend fiberglass mounts today instead of skin mounts. Simply take a length and girth measurement and a few good color photos and release the fish. Send the measurements to the taxidermist along with the photos and he'll have a replica back to you quickly.

Fiberglass mounts are actually the most practical and easiest to plan for. A skin-mount prize to cherish for a lifetime needs careful handling from the time you set the hook. You need not worry about keeping the fish in good condition, freezing it or shipping it. In addition, fiberglass mounts last much longer than the old-style skin mounts.

It's difficult, if not impossible, to tell the difference between a skin-mount and a fiberglass mount. When the taxidermist has performed his magic, your big crappie will again be the beautiful trophy for which you searched years. Whether you intend to mount it or release it, proper handling of the crappie is important.

Chapter 9

HOW TO FIND GOOD SPOTS

When most anglers look at a lake, they see the obvious surface structure and the land mass along the shoreline. Where should one start their search for the sometimes elusive crappie? That's a good question that, unfortunately, many anglers don't even bother to consider.

Those unfamiliar with the lake may start out at the nearest shoreline. Such a random approach, however, may be the slowest way to locate a good fishing spot. In the summer, crappie may be in deeper water away from the shoreline. At other times of year, a shallow approach may be the key.

Toledo Bend guide, John Dean, chases bass and crappie on the big lake along the Texas/Louisiana border and has for many years. He has developed patterns for catching crappie over most of the year.

In the late summer, for example, reservoir crappie will typically be in the feeder creek channels close to deep river edges. They'll often hold there until springtime rolls around again. The best areas, according to Dean, may be half to 3/4 of the way back into a distinct creek channel.

Look for bends with a lot of timber or other cover on them, he suggests. Then use a depth finder to check out the depths for fish.

A little later, in the fall, incoming fresh water from rainshowers could move reservoir fish from the far reaches in the back of a creek to the front of it. Any kind of brush should hold the crappie then throughout the winter. When spring arrives, the fish will scatter and move shallow to spawn.

In the spring, crappie move shallow to spawn on sandy spots commonly found on the secondary points on the inside edge of a grassline, like hydrilla or coontail moss. When the water temperature is 65 to 72 degrees, crappie are bedding up. After performing their duties, the guide finds them moving to the outer edge of grasslines.

One May on Toledo Bend, Dean found a half dozen areas where an average of 50 crappie could be taken each morning and 100 crappie each evening. The fish were located on main lake points of grassbeds, anywhere the hydrilla came to a point under water. The grass following the contour of the bottom and so did the post-spawn crappie.

The successful anglers were tossing 1/32-ounce tube jigs on top of the hydrilla and working it off the edge. As the jigs was falling, suspended crappie would strike the lures near the bottom. They caught crappie between 3/4 and 1 1/2 pounds almost every cast.

Forty Thousand Crappie

Dean and his clients, and six or seven other crappie-fishing boats, did this for six straight weeks at one grass bed. He figures that there must have been 1,000 crappie caught there every day during that period. That's a super spot!

"When the fish get through spawning, they move out toward the main lake to the outside edge of the grass in 15 feet of water and hold there," Dean explains. "When water temperatures start getting hot in the summertime, they'll move on to the deep creeks. That's when and where night fishing for crappie begins to dominate the action."

Right now, the after-dark angling is difficult to top, but another option is the tailrace waters below dams. Crappie can be congregated below the dams, along with a variety of other fish.

Those unfamiliar with the lake may start out at the nearest shoreline. Such a random approach, however, may be the slowest way to locate a good fishing spot.

They move upstream because of the resulting increase in oxygen and the obvious smorgasbord of forage available beneath the dams.

When water is being released from the dam, fishing is best. Forage is being served, and a white/pearl or yellow lead-head jig, such as Blakemore's Road Runner Turbo Tail, is a great crappie producer. Use a 1/16 ounce jig and toss to the slower moving currents and those eddies or pockets of calm water available. The small spinner blade on the Road Runner helps attract strikes in the turbulent water.

If the flow is just too fast to get the jigs down, try putting two in tandem. Tie the first to the end of the line and a second of a different color to a 12-inch dropper line. Position the dropper about 18 inches above the bottom jig. A lightweight spinning or spincasting outfit with 6 to 8 pound test line will cast the fare without many problems.

Those without a boat can fish the tailrace area from the bank below the dam or spillway. You'll probably need plenty of jigs since these areas have plenty of lure-snatching riprap. Drift the lures into the quieter stretches of the tailrace, and keep the line taut to minimize hangups. Letting the current put a belly in your line will allow your bait to drop under a rock on the bottom.

Follow The Forage

Another way for boaters to locate good crappie spots year around involves the use of a depth finder. It is a fast way of covering a lot of water. Using the electronics to locate not the crappie, but the baitfish on which they feed is the key. Schools of "specks" depend on sizable quantities of minnows and other forage such as grass shrimp, so finding a good source for their dining requirements can pay big dividends.

Threadfin shad are found in many parts of the country (primarily below the Mason-Dixon line), and they are a prime crappie forage when available. Clouds of shad minnows can be detected on a good LCD or flasher. They often stretch for hundreds of feet and are a lot easier to see on a screen than the inverted "V" that may mark individual fish. Shad presence is evidence that the water temperature and oxygen levels are right for crappie as well.

Move the boat through waters eight feet or deeper with your eyes on the locator. Switch back over the slightly deeper basins carved into the bottom until you locate the schools of forage. It may take an hour of such looking to find the better areas with plenty of food for the crappie. The real key to discovering the best area is to continue the search until the masses of forage has been located.

Once you have found the "promised land," then place your minnows or jigs at that depth and slowly drift through the area. Use your trolling motor is no wind is present to check out the immediate area. If your scouting is on target, so will be your catch!

Chapter 10

FISHING IN THE GRASS

"They ought to be here in this grass," smiled my guide. "A friend and I caught a hundred yesterday!"

My new acquaintance from Ohio and I were inside a perimeter of heavy weed growth which obstructed our view of Lake Griffin in Central Florida. We were well behind the tall vegetation, and out of sight of any fishermen motoring by. Between us and the shore were more weeds, generally sawgrass and arrowhead. This spot should be a secret, I thought.

John Harmon, an expert crappie fisherman who seeks warmer weather and southern crappie for about six months each year, instructed me on his technique for hooking small minnows. He uses a small bobber and split shot attached to six pound test monofilament above a No. 6 or 8 hook. A light wire hook is employed and placed right through one eye of the baitfish and out the other.

"They'll live longer this way," said the retired GM plant worker. "It'll help keep them out of grass entanglements."

A 16-foot long cane pole is used to drop the minnow in the sparse, open areas around the boat. For an angler used to conventional gear, the cane pole rig is a unique and enjoyable break from casting. For crappie and other panfish in the grass, it is an effective way to fish.

Harmon spends a lot of time on the water each year fishing for crappie in and around vegetation. He is one of the best weed fishermen around, and my purpose for the trip was to pick his brains on his successful technique. John frequently comes back to a marina with a basket full of the frying morsels, and he didn't mind helping out a visiting angler by showing me where to locate grass-bound crappie.

Emergent Vegetation

John had cane poles and a few dozen small minnows stowed in his aluminum boat ready to go that morning. John and I motored over to an area of emergent vegetation and pulled inside the reeds into a small clearing. Crappie in many southern natural lakes and ponds move into the weedy shallows on each full moon in the spring to spawn. The best times to find such fish are normally between mid February and mid May, depending on latitude, weather and water conditions.

"Regardless of the lake you are on, you'll find that the males come in first," says John. "You can catch them in these weeds all day. Then, when the females come into the bedding area, that's all you will catch - females."

In the following two hours we caught from that spot about 25 crappie weighing about a pound. Most were taken on the minnows, but we were able to take a few from the open pockets with small spinners on an ultralight spinning outfit. The action was slow, according to John. The fish had moved back out and would return that evening, perhaps.

Heavy vegetation is an excellent area for crappie any time of the year. Knowing where to look in the grassy areas is essential for filling a wire basket with the pan-sized morsels.

Productive spots may vary seasonally, though, so a local "guide" is often advisable on unfamiliar waters.

"Specs like to spawn on sandy bottoms near grassy cover," John points out. "I look for the light green shoreline areas. The smaller light green trees grow in the shallow swampy areas with sandy bottoms needed for the spawning fish. Areas with

In two hours we caught from that spot about 25 crappie weighing about a pound. Most were taken on the minnows, but we were able to take a few from the open pockets with small spinners on an ultralight spinning outfit. The action was slow, according to John.

hardwoods, that is the big oaks, are not as productive for the specks'', he adds.

There are equally good methods to catch crappie in deeper, vegetated waters. In fact, my first episode with weed loving crappie occurred several years ago. We were fishing a reservoir for bass that morning and found fishing to be very slow. We had caught only two small fish when my partner suggested we move into the submerged trees, and try a relatively little-known method for crappie action.

Scooping Holes In The Canopy

Neither of us had tried jigging small jig and grub combinations in holes in the matted vegetation before, but we were game for anything. We moved off the flats into the old river channel which was jammed with floating aquatic weeds. After motoring through a couple of bends, we nosed the bass boat into the partially submerged trees which lined the old river bank. A floating mass of vegetation had clogged up the trees off the channel itself, and our boat parted them as we slid in among them.

After coasting to a stop, we were surrounded by floating cover and trees. We then scooped "holes" in the floating weeds with our paddle, and dropped our jigs through them. I lifted the rod tip, moving the small jig off the bottom. It stopped. A swift upward movement of the rod set the hook and I continued to lift upward as the fish made off to the side. As he approached the hole, he became entangled in the heavy root structure of the floating plants, so I heaved both the 1 1/2 pound crappie and the hyacinth plant into the boat.

I dropped him in the live well and grabbed the paddle to scoop out the hole again. I moved it back and forth, creating another hole in the bed of floating vegetation and again dropped the 1/32 ounce jig into it. After four or five rod twitches, a fish grabbed it and took off. This time the fish came straight up from the eight feet of water and through the hole as I flipped him into the boat. I dropped the 3/4 pound crappie into the livewell.

Within ten minutes, my fishing partner had three more crappie, including a fat one-pounder. My hole had 'dried' up so I paddled out another on the other side of the boat. After missing two strikes, I finally added a hand-sized crappie to our mess. When action slowed again, we backed out of the weed jam and moved down the river channel 20 yards. We both scooped out holes near the bow and began jigging again.

My partner's rod buckled sharply as the tip plunged into the hole while he tried desperately to gain back the momentum. "Pow!" went the 10-pound test line as the punishment of an

As holes are scooped out and the plants are separated, food is dislodged from it and falls to the bottom where the fish are waiting. Any surface disturbance will knock small bugs, worms, insect larvae, etc. into the water and baitfish or crappie won't be far behind.

obvious lunker bass was just too much for the monofilament. We added a crappie and a bluegill to our bag before moving again.

We found that getting the lure to descend was sometimes a problem due to the hair-like roots of the plants which sometimes extend a foot below and to the side of each plant. These fibers would cling to each other and prevent the lure from dropping through the hole unless it was scooped out properly. Finally, we got the knack, but realized that a garden rake would do a much better job.

We tried to make the holes about a foot or so in diameter so that we could hoist the fish up without a problem. Many times we caught multiple fish from the same hole. We also found that one hole might really produce while ones adjacent might not at all. Certain areas held better sized fish and some held more of one species than others.

65

Vertical Movement

Slowly jigging the lure up and down provided us with the most control. Vertical travel of a foot or so appeared to be the most productive lure presentation, and this was done within two feet of the bottom. The most productive depth we found was seven to nine feet, although the method worked as shallow as five feet. As is normally the case, the shallower areas held smaller fish and at depths less than four feet we found nothing at all.

We used spinning rigs, spooled with 8 and 10-pound test line and there was no appreciable difference in productivity. Jig size appears to be important, and the 1/32 ounce size results in more strikes. The best grub tail to use may be simply a small 3/4 to 1-inch piece off the tail of a small plastic worm.

The color didn't seem to make much of a difference that day as we caught fish on white, yellow, green and purple grubs. The plain jig with grub trailer was a much better lure than some small maribou jigs which we also tried. On some trips since then, I've had to resort to cutting off the nylon, hair or maribou tail of old crappie jigs to use with the plastic tail I prefer.

Engine noise doesn't appear to affect the fish. I normally shut off the outboard after the bow of my boat drifts to a stop by the floating bed of hyacinths and have caught fish as soon as my jig nears the bottom. Even if I am sitting 20 feet inside a bed and want to move another 15 feet deeper into a weed-clogged forest, I'll crank up the motor, evidently without disturbing the fish.

The reason that this method works is simple. As holes are scooped out and the plants are separated, food is dislodged and falls to the bottom where the fish are waiting for small bugs, worms, insect larvae, etc. Food is everywhere under the floating canopy, and it attracts and holds crappie.

Many southern waters abound with productive floating cover and other aquatic weed masses rooted to the shoreline. The floating variety are the easiest to use this method on, but it will work on hydrilla, coontail and other rooted plants. Just find some vegetation and fish it. You should catch crappie!

Chapter 11

'STRUCTURE' YOUR FISHING

There is certainly a lot to learn about finding productive fishing areas anywhere, and a successful crappie angler must have the desire and determination to want to learn. Reading, studying and then getting out on the water and practicing is the best method to success. Putting facts to use at the right time is what makes good fishermen.

The importance of structure was proven to me years ago. As I descended down the anchor rope 50 feet into the deep, dark depths of the Atlantic Ocean, I wondered what the reef would really look like. Four foot waves were tossing the boat around a bit and the underwater surge was very present as I made my way down to the reef.

When I reached the bottom I found the anchor was gingerly grasping only the sand. There was no reef in sight, only sand as far as I could see. I swam around for another 10 minutes looking for proof of the reef that I thought was there. But, I never found it.

The chart recorder aboard the boat had, we interpreted, marked a small three-foot tall reef structure, but not only was there no coral, there was not a single fish. The fact that most fish are found only on structure could not have been made clearer.

I returned to the boat very disappointed and began looking again for a reef. Soon, I spotted a true ledge on the chart recorder and anchored. This time, when I descended, the reef was quickly discovered. On it where thousands of fish. The schools of fish were a sharp contrast to the barren sand encountered earlier. The word "structure" really took on new meaning.

But what does thousands of salt water fish on a reef mean to the freshwater crappie fishermen?

Freshwater fish relate to cover exactly as do the salty ones. Several additional dives in inland lakes and rivers have proven this to me. Talking to other successful fishermen and catching schools of fat crappie off structure myself have also shown this to be true.

Deep Water And Cover

Schools of large fish prefer deeper water and the presence of some form of cover. I am sure that many fishermen have caught bigger crappie and at deeper depths which support that particular fact. There will also be some who have caught large specks in the shallows while they were not spawning. It does happen and there are several parameters which dictate that happening to some extent.

To think, though, that crappie prefer to be in shallow water is incorrect. If you or I were standing in the lake, we would want to be in the shallows near safety, which for us is dry land. Similarly, the fish is at the outskirts of his environment while in shallow water.

For most finny creatures, safety and protection lies 180 degrees from ours. The crappie will retreat to deep water and spend most of their time there, just as we spend most of our time on dry land. That's where we feel most comfortable.

The only time large crappie spend any length of time at all in the shallows with minimal cover is when they are spawning.

This is strictly a biological urge. When specks begin their spawning activities, they become very protective of their shallow water nest and will not move far from it.

Freshwater fish relate to cover exactly as do the salty ones. Talking to other successful fishermen and catching schools of fat crappie off structure myself have also shown this to be true.

Down Under

I had an interesting SCUBA diving experience in a small lake one January a few years ago. It was spawning period and several male specks had fanned debris away from their nest in three feet of water near the edge of a dropoff. Most of the nests were on part of an island near the lake's midsection.

The barrow pit was a man-made lake dug for fill dirt. The banks were deep and cut in a straight line. That is probably why most of the spawning crappie were drawn to the shallow shores and cattails around the island. The lake was exceptionally clear, with ten to 15 feet visibility and heavy vegetation growth in the shallows.

The beds were all located in the light outside stalks about five feet from the drop off. I descended to about seven feet and moved along in the deeper water, keeping the shallows at eye level in front of me. The first bed I noticed had a crappie of about one pound on it. As I approached slowly, he moved off and retreated four feet to the rear toward the island.

When I neared the bed he stood his ground keeping me straight in front of him. He seemed to just 'hover' there, keeping

69

If fish do not get smarter as they get older, then why do many anglers catch only the small ones and not the lunkers? The reason is because the larger crappie are in deeper water than most people fish. The schools of small fish can often be found in shallower water, but the bigger slabs seldom are.

an eye on me. I stuck out my hand over the bed and wiggled my finger. He moved forward slightly, stopping a few feet away from the bed and my hand.

The speck wasn't about to desert the nest. A similar happening occurred at another bed as I moved along the island's perimeter.

At first sighting, most of the crappie would move away from the bed four or five feet, then as I moved by they would come back. All were very stubborn about leaving. Their need to protect the nest was strong.

For me, it was a very interesting and informative dive. This experience taught me something about crappie behavior during their spawning activities, but I would certainly not conclude similar responses during the summer, fall and winter. I'm relatively sure that they would move to cover in the deep water of that lake.

Big, Smart Fish?

If fish do not get smarter as they get older, then why do many anglers catch only the small ones and not the lunkers? The reason is because the larger crappie are in deeper water than most people fish. The schools of small fish can often be found in shallower water, but the bigger slabs seldom are.

The size distribution is much better than you would think. To look at most stringers of crappie, for example, one would think that there was only one fish weighing more than one pound for each 100 fish weighing less. Not so! Many larger, deep water specks are seldom fished for and die of old age.

Why also are there five times as many big crappie caught in the spawning months than during the rest of the year? Because the bigger fish are shallow and more prone to being caught at this time of the year.

The larger crappie are usually females, but they are not necessarily smarter than the smaller males. They simply want more protection, and thus, depth and structure, than the schools of yearlings which cruise shallower waters.

Most states throughout the country have waters with several excellent types of crappie structure, both man made and natural. In about 10 percent of the many lakes I have fished, I've found sunken boats and specks love them. The boats have been shipwrecked, deserted and usually are completely submerged. Almost all will hold fish and I never overlook a sunken object when I come across one.

Of course, big specks also prefer cover that nature made. Aquatic vegetation, brush piles, rock formations and other structure attract crappie.

Chapter 12

UNDER THE PLANKS

I stumbled on my first concentration of dock crappie when I was in high school. At the time, I did not have a boat, so I was relegated to shore. The small sand pit in southeastern Kansas had yielded numerous panfish and bass to earlier expeditions with light spinning tackle. The sole dock was a long walk from the car, and I seldom fished it.

A relatively slow day and an adventurous spirit led me to the dock on the far side of the pit. I stood beside the walking pier and made a long cast with the tiny 1/16 ounce jig. As soon as it touched down beside the main dock platform, I had my first crappie. Twenty casts later, I had at least a dozen on my stringer. All had come from under the dock to sock my little jig.

My fishing partner quickly decided to join in the action and walked over from the unproductive side of the lake. After a short while and numerous crappie, we dragged our stringer on the ground as we walked out of the sand pit. I left with a lot of fish cleaning to do and a lesson about the effectiveness of fishing for crappie under docks.

Floating docks and fixed piers are two of the more common man-made crappie haunts. They exist on most waters and are a favorite spot of many panfishermen. Some waters abound with this type of crappie habitat. Those lakes whose shorelines are crowded with residences usually offer numerous dock structure.

Lakefront owners often build better access in the form of long docks on their waters.

Docks, whether for fishing or loading a boat, come in a variety of shapes and sizes. Some have boat houses or small cabins built on the end, and others are no wider at their terminal point than is their gangway from shore. The lengths and conditions of the docks also vary greatly. Some are little more than a bulkhead extension, while others are several hundred feet long reaching far out from shore. There are always some docks that are partially dilapidated, and occasionally, unweathered pilings and cross-members denote a relatively new addition to the "waterscape." Most are wooden, but a few metal piers and posts can occasionally be found.

Some docks float in waters 20 feet deep and others are piling-supported piers primarily in a marsh. Deep water is, however, relative to the type of lake you're fishing, and waters deep enough to concentrate crappie could be just six feet. Other than during the spawning season, the dock should have a minimum of six feet of water beneath it in order to attract crappie.

While those docks and piers located in deep water often are the most productive year around crappie haunts, other factors may dictate just how productive such a structure is. The best deep-water dock in which to discover a school of resident crappie depends on several physical things.

Shade And Entanglement

Crappie love shade. That is quickly apparent to the scuba diver that peers beneath the planks of a deep water dock. I once noticed a school of probably 200 under a floating platform that was only 10 feet by 10 feet. I swam around and through the "ball" of crappie. They parted with my approach and pulled back tightly together.

Probably the most important feature to look for in selecting a pier or dock is the amount of shade. Piers with a house, gazebo, boat shed or other large structure on their ends in deep water are excellent. The wider piers and docks which cast wider shadows

Marine growth on the pier supports is evidence of the food cycle and provides an opportunity for catching a few crappie. The larger diameter posts are also good protection for the crappie and their forage.

are prime territories for a school of crappie. A long, "skinny" pier in shallow water offers relatively few forage opportunities and in most cases, is a waste of time for the crappie angler.

Another key factor in the suitability of docks for harboring a concentration of crappie is the density and size of the support posts beneath the pier. The more dense the man-made structure (number of posts, cross-members near the water, etc.), the more productive a dock or pier can be. Forage is one of the key ingredients in a productive dock.

Pilings that support piers provide food and cover the entire height of the "water column." Minnows, grass shrimp and crustaceans feed on the small plankton, and crappie and other predator fish feed on them. Marine growth on the pier supports is evidence of the food cycle and an opportunity for catching a few crappie. The larger diameter posts also provide good

75

protection for the crappie and their forage, and they are much better fish habitat than the smaller pilings.

Most experienced crappie anglers search for docks and piers offering the fish the most protection possible. The more comfort provided crappie and their forage, the better the fishing will be. The same principal considerations in selecting a pile-supported dock also apply to floating docks. The best will have abundant forage, be near deep water, and will be large enough to provide considerable shade and protection.

Habitat Supplements

The composition of the bottom at the base of the dock and around it is a variable that should also be considered. Submerged trees, brush and other man-made structure can often be discovered lying on the lake bed directly below the docks. Such supplemental habitat is normally placed near docks by shoreside land owners. They do their structural introductions in order to establish a holding area for crappie and other game fish beneath their docks.

Anglers finding submerged habitat can often enjoy a productive fishing trip. Other things lying at or near the end of the dock could be crab or minnow traps. Many dock owners like to have a supply of baitfish or good eatin' at the end of the planks ready for the plucking. Traps are utilized extensively in the south to capture minnows for both set lines and sport fishing.

Small baitfish such as shiners, chubsuckers, potguts and other minnows are normally drawn to the dock-placed traps by a chum. The chum may be bread dough, wheat or some other grain product which is scattered in the trap area to attract the forage. Obviously, since forage is numerous in and around these traps, so are crappie and other predators. Crappie anglers will be wise to fish such structures for their prey. Crappie are generally found near a good food source, so the chummed area that provides forage is a good place to focus your fishing.

Boat control is important when fishing piers and docks. Any current through them can result in a boat being bumped against the structure disturbing the fish below. Usually, the most productive way to approach the dock is to fish it starting nearest the bank. The successful lure angler may have to cast several times to the same general area before enticing a strike.

At the end of the dock, circle it and cast the perimeter. If the water is deep, use a depth finder to check out the bottom for any "plantings" of traps, brush, etc.

You may also find structure below the water that once stood above it. Almost any man-made object that was built to be above the water's surface will provide good habitat for crappie once it is lying on the bottom. Old piers, wood pilings, buildings over water and docks often deteriorate and fall into the waters beneath. New structures are sometimes put up beside the original docks with little regard for cleaning out the dilapidated cross-members and wood below the surface.

When major piers collapse, the submerged maze of supports can be difficult to fish. Hangups are a reality, but the crappie fishing can be exceptional. Many fallen man-made structures have timber going in different directions beneath the surface, and the crappie love such places. They can move in and out of the "condominiums" at will, when in fear of larger predators or when after forage.

Dock Tactics

Evie Moreland, of Fruitland Park, Florida, often fishes the man-made structures on the Harris Chain of Lakes in the central part of the state. He opts for small minnows, about an inch long, fished near the bottom and will employ an armful of cane poles to spread out around the boat. The former manager of the Twin Palms Resort and Fish Camp on Lake Griffin has developed effective patterns to catch larger crappie.

He will normally set his baits at different depths until he finds where they are feeding. Then, he'll set his bobbers at that productive depth. His hooks are normally a number 1 or a 1/0, which is relatively large for crappie. A number 4 split shot and a 15 foot section of 14 to 17 pound test monofilament line complete Moreland's standard rig. This rig is particularly effective late in the evening when he is often anchored and still-fishing. The fish move in toward shore to feed at that time, according to Moreland, and that time period from 5 p.m. until dark is usually the best time for big dock crappie.

Many panfishermen spend too much time in open water. They may venture into shallower areas only in the spring. Time wasted, though, on unproductive waters could be better spent checking out the piers and docks for the right habitat to attract crappie. Those anglers that work hard to establish a dock pattern will often be productive. If they establish the pattern early in the day, most crappie chasers will end up with a sizable catch.

Dock and pier structures are often excellent crappie haunts, and they yield lots of fish to the knowledgeable angler. Such man-made cover can often be just right for a school of crappie!

Chapter 13

DIGGING FOR
SPECK ACTION

The small jig moved sideways as the retrieve brought it near the submerged rock outcropping. A small, half-pound crappie swam sideward with the minnow fake. I quickly reeled the fish to the boat and lifted him aboard.

That was my first speck of the day and it took me some two hours to find him. Other boats on the waters were having similar problems. I continued to toss the silver jig along the tree-lined banks and over the rock piles which were visible only through my Polaroid sunglasses.

Finally, I was able to snag a fat one and three-quarter pounder off an island point in the reclaimed phosphate pit. We maneuvered the boat through the cuts and channels, around the islands and across the various points that were found in Lake Two on the Tenoroc Fish Management Area.

We were about to give up hope for catching a nice mess that morning when a cast near an overhanging tree resulted in a sharp bow of my rod. I set the hook, thinking that it might be a bass. The strong two-pound crappie was subdued, and, with renewed hope,

I made as many casts as I could in the following 30 minutes, along the overhanging banks and in a small canal adjacent to the boat ramp. Another one-and-one-half-pound crappie was all that I could muster.

It was not a typical day on the Florida pits. Those who caught a few crappie definitely had to work for them, and after four hours of casting, several of the anglers in that particular pit were fishless. Fishing can be like that occasionally, but fortunately it is usually the opposite experience.

Normally, a bagfull of specks is easier to catch in a pit than in any other body of water. Previous to this, at another Lakeland phosphate pit, we had little trouble in catching 50 crappie in the same time span. The fish probably averaged a pound, and those results were not typical either.

A normal day on a Florida phosphate pit over five hours of fishing usually results in 10 to 15 crappie, which is well above the average production from most other waters in the state of Florida. The Game and Fresh Water Fish Commission has verified through creel samplings that pit fishing is more productive than fishing the natural lakes, on a fish-per-hour basis.

The Tenoroc State Reserve provides good fishing often in the nine pits that are open to the public on a permit basis. The lakes at Tenoroc vary considerably, but are fairly typical of most phosphate pits. Some are pastureland-type waters with very little shoreline cover, while others are completely unreclaimed and provide craggy outcroppings, heavy brush and trees along the shoreline and rocks jutting above the surface in various spots.

Irregular Shorelines

Most pits around the country have an irregular shoreline and offer steep banks to cast toward. Very few shallow areas are found in the pits, and because of that, aquatic vegetation is normally minimal. Waters in most pits are of medium clarity, but occasionally, a pit can be found with fairly clear water. Many have rocks, sand and gravel outcroppings along their bottoms.

All the pits are different in structure present. Some have vast pad beds, others cattails and bulrushes and still others are nearly void of emergent vegetation.

The unique pit structure are places that crappie become adapted to quickly. It is not normal habitat for the lake-bound fish, but it is something they can relate to easily.

Brush structure is abundant along the lake bottom in many pits, and ordinarily vegetation grows profusely before a pit is flooded. Once inundated, it provides excellent cover for the entire food chain, from phytoplankton right on up to the predator fish.

Many pits produce crappie of one and one-half to two pounds, but seldom does the word get out as to which pit the fish was caught in. The lucky anglers are usually pretty tight-lipped about that. Pits offer a great opportunity for anglers with structure knowledge and techniques. Underwater structure in the form of submerged humps, dragline channels, rock piles, etc., provide fishable cover away from the shoreline.

While many anglers are uncomfortable casting to open water and the structure beneath, the good fishermen find these type areas to be a real blessing.

The large mining and processing firms are the leaders in creating these new sport fish waters when restoring those pits that they are through digging in. The mining companies are following stringent government regulations as they reclaim the land. Nature does its share of the work to green up the shorelines and numerous islands creating excellent habitat for the food chain that normally blossoms in the highly enriched waters.

All the pits are different in structure present. Some have vast pad beds, others cattails and bulrushes and still others are nearly void of emergent vegetation. Some of the better ones have a profuse growth of hydrilla. Many have sharp dropoffs near some banks while some pits still have "mountains" on the perimeter.

Optimal Depths

There may be literally a thousand different shorelines on the various pits. But the better ones for "specks" have plenty of deep water and structural characteristics. Submerged rock piles and humps are locations of super fishing for pit crappie.

A depth finder is often required to find such, and the Lowrance X-16 basically "empties the water out of a pit" to give you a great view of the bottom structure. The programmable chart recorder lets you set the scale, be it 0 to 40 feet, 0 to 10 feet or 30 to 40 feet (to inspect only the water just off the bottom if in 37 or 38-foot depths).

Control structures exist on the pits to regulate water levels and the spillways and culverts with flowage are hot spots for feeding crappie. The bottom is generally carved out beneath such discharges and the crappie often lie off to the side of the fast water looking for forage.

Strips of submerged "islands" are often left by the dragline operation and these areas are excellent places for a school of crappie to corner their prey. Grown-over islands exist and deep water 'cuts' in the islands are excellent spots to fish, since crappie will often suspend off such places to await a school of baitfish.

Jigs are often the most effective bait to toss in man-made waters. White hued maribou jigs are highly successful in many phosphate pits around the country.

Local anglers that fish some of the hard to reach pits in the area find excellent crappie angling. Many catches of 50 crappie weighing up to two pounds are reported. Some supposedly have "wall-to-wall" crappie, mostly in the one-half pound range, while other have smaller schools contained larger fish.

One of the better pits that I know of offers several submerged shelf running from seven feet down to 20 feet of water on either side. Big fish were a strong possibility there until word got out about the average catch. Numerous locals trying to get in on the fantastic quality and quantity flocked to the lake and almost cleaned it out.

Many huge stringers were carried off day after day for the following two months. The word was soon out that the pit no longer had crappie left. Good anglers still went in and caught fish, but the onslaught had taken its toll.

83

The experienced crappie fishermen often catch 25 to 50 crappie on a pit visit, but they often have to work at it. They have to fish several areas and establish a pattern initially that will be successful throughout the lake around similar types of cover. Those anglers that can find the honey hole where they can catch fish on successive casts literally have it made.

Effective Bait for Pits

The most productive baits in a pit usually depend on the particular water. In terms of success/productivity, many pits are 'minnow pits,' meaning that live bait in that form catches the most specks.

Other pits are "jig pits" where small jigs are the most effective bait to toss. White hued maribou jigs are highly successful in many phosphate pit waters around the country.

Naturally, various styles and color combinations are effective under certain conditions. While the pH level of phosphate-excavated waters varies considerably from pit to pit, from very acidic to very alkaline, the scent products appear to work in all types of water.

Fishing in the phosphate pits can be a year-round, productive activity. Due to the extreme depths of the pits, water condition fluctuations are fairly immune to the effects of winds and weather.

Cold fronts and heat waves affect the pits much less than they do the shallow, natural bodies of water. While the fish may be "turned off" in the natural lakes and streams, crappie in the pits may be on a feeding binge. A good angler may want to look deeper for cold water crappie at times other than when they're spawning, but if he knows where to search and uses the right equipment, he'll find them.

Structure techniques successfully utilized in impoundments throughout the U.S. are effective on the pits. Live bait, jigs, small crankbaits and spinners are successful lures in these waters. The schools of crappie that chase small shad around the pits are suckers for such fare.

Thousands of watercraft are car-topped and trailered to the numerous pits and other man-made waters around the country. The lightweight rigs are easy to put in on the pits, which seldom have a launch ramp. The small craft generally use a trolling motor to maneuver and it is sufficient. Man-made waters are abundant in many areas, yet they receive no attention other than from locals. Irrigation canals, barrow pits for highway fill, and even small reservoirs also frequently provide great crappie fishing.

An angler can often double his catch rate in pits. Crappie seem to grow faster and chunkier, since forage is abundant in the little impoundments.

Chapter 14

HOT WATER CRAPPIE

Pick a lake or river in your state that provides excellent year 'round angling for big crappie, and chances are that a thermal effluent flows into from either a coal fired or a nuclear power plant.

While winter and early spring do bring on the best angling for large "slabs," February, March and April tend to be the favorite months for many fishermen. Crappie abound in many power plant waters, and fishing in the cooling ponds generally remains "hot" throughout the year.

Speck fishing can be great, even in the very hottest months. Crappie may be on the prowl after minnows more often in the summer and fall months when that forage is most available.

Due to the pretty much ideal situations of heated water and more constant water characteristics, such as pH, temperature, etc., and water level year around, growth of sport fish is phenomenal. The cooling reservoir provides a year round growing season for crappie, which increases the probability of their obtaining lunker proportions.

Variations of pH are minimal and the annual warm water temperatures and nutrient level in these impoundments encourage growth of small organisms. That benefits the food chain all the way to the top predators. Heated reservoirs are normally full of forage.

Establishing special size and bag limits and closing off a portion of the reservoir to provide a sanctuary for the fish are management policies of many fish and game agencies. Some have implemented a stocking program of threadfin shad on heated reservoirs to provide additional forage. The threadfin shad has experienced exceptional survival and reproductive rates.

Temperatures And Oxygen

Water temperature and oxygen content are also key elements in heated waters offering excellent angling. As the water temperature increases, oxygen content decreases and crappie metabolism increases to a certain point. The oxygen requirements of a large crappie, for instance, increase dramatically in 80 degree water, as opposed to 45 degree water. Internal body functions react to the elevated temperatures and activity increases.

Research has shown that a more active fish requires more oxygen until the water temperature reaches approximately 85 degrees. The activity rapidly declines above that mark resulting in less requirements for dissolved oxygen. Since most fish appear to be quite comfortable in even 80 degree water, year 'round angling opportunities are available in the heated waters of various southern power plants.

Nuclear power facilities, which are abundant throughout the south, may use water from the reservoir for cooling the reactor. Inlet waters are run through turbines to produce the power, then through a condenser and treating cycle before being discharged back into the lake. In the process, the effluent is heated causing a warming of the reservoir.

Similarly, water is normally extracted from a cooling pond to cool a fossil fuel power generating plant and returned to the lake at a much higher temperature. The effluent of both types of power plants is closely monitored by the EPA and NRC to assure compliance with local, state and national pollution standards.

Various reports have shown the heated effluent has no harmful effect on a fishery. It may, in fact, be very beneficial by

The winter temperature of heated reservoirs is located near the warm water source and along the circulating channel. Most heated waters average 10 degrees warmer than other lakes around the region.

providing additional forage growth for fattening up the fish. The greater abundance of food attracts predator fish and enables their faster growth.

Locating The Big Specks

To find some of the big crappie, an angler should follow the currents which move the food supply around. Moving schools after forage should be located and fished to creel a good limit. The successful fishermen observe current patterns and follow the forage.

Warm water bays and outlets harbor much of the small shad and minnow forage and, in doing so, attract the game fish. "Warming" agents such as cattails and moss beds can influence thermal effects to a lesser extent and may aid in patterning fish.

89

A spring or cool water source is important for summertime anglers when lake temperatures in the discharge canal can reach very high levels. When the cooling units are not functioning, the discharge water will be the same temperature as the nearby lake waters. Crappie will not congregate in such areas, so a move off to deep water is in order for the productive fisherman.

The majority of the heated waters offer good angling for crappie and either stripers or hybrid striped bass. Since many power plant impoundments are forage-intensive, the opportunity for the predator heavyweights exists. Likewise, the chances of good angling for those predators are excellent.

Small threadfin shad is the common forage of big crappie in the hot water lakes, and lures resembling those baitfish are always good. As a caveat, though, a few power plant waters have such an abundance of forage that the angler's quarry is often full and not in a biting mood.

Thermal Differences

The winter temperature of heated reservoirs is located near the warm water source and along the circulating channel. Most heated waters average 10 degrees warmer than other lakes around the region.

An elevated temperature during the cold season on power plant lakes mean less winter kill of the forage fish which are also localized near the warm water source. On some of the existing cooling reservoirs, officials are adding more generating units and this makes the water even hotter. When they heat up the waters, that speeds up the metabolism of the fish.

When the metabolic rate is up, crappie eat more to sustain their higher energy level. They grow larger and faster, but then again, their aging process is faster too. On some lakes, you can easily feel the heat coming from the body of a freshly caught fish.

Maximum cool weather forage is available to power plant predators in February/March as the early hatch of shad often fattens them. For the rest of the year, prior to the winter kill in November, forage is abundant.

Prime Locations

Nearly 100 cooling or power plant reservoirs exist in the southern region of the U.S. Texas has, by far, the most, with almost 40 heated reservoirs, while Alabama, North Carolina and Tennessee all have at least eight. Most of the other states have at least four within their borders.

Several of the heated waters are not household names, but most offer good angling opportunities. Some of their better catches may even surprise you. Consider those waters that might offer excellent fishing for cool weather crappie.

Many of the power plant waters are tops in their state for crappie. Noted for great crappie angling are the 11,200-acre Neely Henry Lake near Gadsden, Alabama; Georgia's popular Lake Sinclair; Arkansas' 36,000-acre Dardanelle impoundment and Georgia's Altamaha River discharge near Baxley.

Heated public waters in Texas that yield good crappie catches are lakes Monticello and Welsh, small power plant cooling reservoirs near Mount Pleasant. Several other 'hot' reservoirs for speck action would include Calaveras, Braunig and Fayette County locations.

Several of the heated waters in Texas currently have special limits and/or regulations imposed to protect the fishery. With the amount of fishing pressure that most receive, the lakes still produce more big crappie than do non-heated waters. Even with several hundred boats on the lake's 2,000 acres each day, Monticello yields lots of large crappie with surprising regularity.

Other good holes include Alabama Power Co. reservoir, Lay Lake, the expansive 30,000-acre Lake Norman in North Carolina, Oklahoma's 5,000-acre Sooner Lake, Kentucky's Herrington Lake, Barkley Lake and Watts Bar Lake in Tennessee and Virginia's Lake Anna.

Most of the southern state's heated waters provide ample opportunity throughout the year to catch some very nice crappie. The effect of an elevated water temperature on the creel harvest may be more pronounced in the winter and summer on this type of lake.

The basic key to finding fish year around is knowing their reaction the thermal and current effects which impact water characteristics such as oxygen, pH, turbidity, etc., and the resulting behavior of the fish.

Chapter 15

BAYOU BASIN SAC-A-LAIT

Two twitches of the rod tip was all it took for a pan-size crappie to tug back. The small bobber disappeared into the stained swamp water and the wispy rod bent into a hook-shape. I lifted the 3/4 pound fish into the boat and glanced forward at my guide for the day, Charlie Jeanmard. He also was hoisting in a crappie of about the same proportions.

Ten fish in the first 15 minutes. Not a bad start, I thought.

"The Sac-a-lait here are not running large enough," stated the veteran crappie fisherman. "We need to move."

For 35 years, the now-retired Lafayette businessman has been fishing the Atchafalaya Basin and catching lots of "sac-a-lait," as the cajuns around the swamp call the crappie. So, who's not to listen to Jeanmard. He used a small hand-held walkie-talkie to tell his friend in a nearby boat that we were moving. Leroy Mouton, his long time fishing companion, agreed that the larger crappie could be elsewhere, so he stowed his rod and followed us.

We motored along the bayou canals through some of the prettiest scenery found in southern Louisiana. We moved through river and creek channels and through cuts that parted a shallow-looking flooded swamp. The depth in the basin, though, can be deceiving. In the swift Atchafalaya River, depths range from 30 to 90 feet, surprisingly deep. Just off the river are numerous

93

Flooded swamps can be dangerous to fish if you don't know what you're doing. When you are fishing in the flooded swamps, you may find that area is only two feet deep. But, in the bayous and tributaries, you can often find 10 to 20 feet of water. The majority of the crappie fishing takes place in the bayous and smaller creeks and canals, away from the deep river channels.

bayous and small tributaries that form the Atchafalaya Basin. The water level back in the basin is always high, according to the locals, and sometimes it is flooded. As a result, plenty of backwater areas exist just from the natural river levels.

The basin is dangerous to fish if you don't know what you're doing. When you are fishing in the flooded swamps, you may find that area is only two feet deep. But, in the bayous and tributaries, you can often find 10 to 20 feet of water. The majority of the crappie fishing takes place in the bayous and smaller creeks and canals, away from the deep river channels.

Jeanmard shut off his outboard and we coasted to a stop along a cypress-lined creek. He readied his 8 1/2 foot rod and

In April, the basin waters are usually high, and crappie are numerous in the marsh areas. If water levels in the basin are low from a relatively dry spring, the crappie will be thick in the basin.

flipped his small jig near the grass-surrounded cypress knees. The tip jerked downward and he swung another palm-size crappie into the boat. My first flip against the overgrown cover just off the bank resulted in an even smaller crappie. We continued to pick up crappie a variety of sizes along the bank.

Finally, Jeanmard caught one that would have easily weighed over a pound; 10 feet further down the bank, my rod was doubled over by a heavy fish. It easily pulled drag from the small Zebco UL 4 reel spooled with six pound test line. I carefully fought the 7 pound drum to the waiting landing net. The tussle was repeated three more times that day with drum almost as large.

Long Jig Poles

The hand-built jig pole worked perfectly on those fish, a couple of catfish, four bass, several sunfish and about 70 crappie ranging up to about 1 1/4 pounds. Jeanmard orders the long, limber graphite rod blanks with a No. 5 or 6 tip and threads the line from the spincast reel through the hollow blank. The reel's function is mostly to hold line and to offer a drag when a larger crappie or other heavy fish is hooked.

Jeanmard's equipment and tactics for the Atchafalaya Basin have evolved from his constant year-round exposure. He and Mouton originally employed small shiner minnows in the basin, but switched to jigs in the early 1970s. Since then, they have used jigs exclusively.

In fact, Jeanmard's daughter makes the area's most popular jigs. Becky's Custom-Made Jigs (204 Ransome St., Lafayette, LA 70501; 318/234-2218) are a hand-tied hair jig with a balanced lead head. They carry 1/64, 1/32 and 1/16 ounce jigs, but Jeanmard prefers the middleweight for springtime action. The 1/64 ounce is also effective on the basin crappie at that time when the fish prefer a smaller jig.

In April, the basin water is usually high, and crappie are numerous outside of the basin, either in the marsh or the Stevenville area. If the water level in the basin is low from a relatively dry spring, the crappie will be thick in the basin.

The Atchafalaya Basin is located south of Interstate 10 and stretches from Lake Arthur to Morgan City, or about 100 miles. The basin is 18 miles at its widest point and is an authentic swamp. When the basin's water is high, most of the swamp is under water. The channels in the basin and swamp are not well marked, so it is advisable to fish with a local or a guide who knows where they are.

"People get lost out there every year," warns Jeanmard in his cajun accent. "You're going into a wild area, so you need to take plenty of gas in your boat and a good map. Those who are unfamiliar with the basin can use their head and a good compass

Crappie like to hang out near some form of cover, according to Jeanmard. He fishes a lot of dropoffs, and uses an LCR to do so. Good sharp dropoffs are best in his opinion, but he'll also keep an eye out for any brush, stumps, or other kind of structure.

to keep from getting lost. A lot of people don't have a compass or don't think about their course, though.''

When crappie are spawning, Jeanmard suggests that you fish the edges of the cover that lies in fairly shallow water. He'll normally use a bobber even in waters two feet deep or less. The fish are normally on the edge in shallow water.

The largest crappie typically taken in the bayous weigh about 2 1/2 pounds, and the limit is usually generous. Jeanmard and Mouton catch a limit just about every time they go fishing, which is three or four times each week. Check out the bayous and remember that good stringers of crappie here will have fish that average one to 1 1/4 pounds!

Bayou Tactics

"We use a combination of black body and chartreuse wing/tail jig in the spring, says Jeanmard. "We use black & orange, blue and white, and black & gray with a tinsel body. The latter is real popular. It's called the minnow. Another good color for fishing in bayous called the bumblebee, is black & yellow."

Another effective tactic for catching Sac-a-lait in the bayous is trolling. The fish often hang out in the middle of the canals for a couple of weeks, but some years that pattern lasts for two or three months. Trolling is the most productive method then.

During years of unusually high water over a long period, the pattern can change. Most bayous are affected by rain runoff, not necessarily that rainfall in the immediate area. The water clarity changes and may get muddy with runoff, particularly if that runoff is through reddish mud country. When that happens, if you can find an area that's clear, you might find some fish. Generally though, the crappie won't be feeding in the muddy areas.

"I like a slightly green color to the water to find fish in," says Jeanmard. "I don't like real clear black water, but I do like it just a little off color. As long as you have four feet of water in a bayou, you're going to find some crappie."

Crappie like to hang out near some form of cover, according to Jeanmard. He fishes a lot of dropoffs, and uses an LCR to do so. Good sharp dropoffs are best in his opinion, but he'll also keep an eye out for any brush, stumps, or other kind of structure.

When fishing around structure in the bayou, good equipment is important. The jig pole outfits that he and his partner use have a drag which is vital when another species feeds on the bait. Jeanmard used a smooth drag to out-fight a 29 pound, 4 ounce buffalo on six pound test recently. It took him about 45 minutes to get the fish to the net.

Weather and Seasons

The wind is not much of a factor in most bayou fishing unless it blows a gale. Fish will bite in the wind or rain. Just before a cold front, the crappie may feed actively, but then after the front moves through, they will normally turn off.

"Then, you can go deeper and try for them, but sometimes they're turned off completely," says the avid bayou angler. "You won't catch as many fish after a front. I prefer the overcast, cloudy days whether fishing shallow or deep. On sunny days, I find you catch the Sac-a-lait early in the morning or late in the day. In the middle of the day, they're not that active."

Chapter 16

ANALYZE THE LAKE

To find crappie, there is nothing better than taking a dip with SCUBA gear and looking for them. On a small Florida lake, a friend and I once explored the depths searching for game fish haunts. The lake was man made and averaged about six feet deep, connecting to a deeper canal. The late-spring dive taught me that post-spawn crappie consider cover more important than deep water.

We scouted the entire lake and canal and found bluegill and largemouth bass present in the heavy cattails and weeds near the shore. The lake was very clear, but a layer of silt covered the bottom up to 15 feet away from the shoreline. I knew the lake had crappie, but we had not located them. As we continued swimming throughout the canal and lake, it became a barren wasteland with no cover of any type.

We saw only a few crappie in the open water as we swam into the deeper 25-foot canal. I noticed something white and shiny in the depths, reflecting the sunlight back toward the glassy surface. I descended and saw that the object was a car sitting on the bottom of the canal. Around the auto and inside it were literally hundreds of crappie. It was the largest school of specks that I have ever seen in an underwater environment.

This structure held the only school of crappie in the 500-acre lake. The auto windows were rolled down, allowing the fish

101

complete access to the interior. It was truly a carload of crappie! The majority of the fish were outside the car, but quickly swam inside or under the vehicle as we approached. The crappie were more at ease with us divers moving through their environment than were other species of fish.

While we can't dive every body of water to locate productive structure for crappie, there are means to stay dry and come up with some likely crappie hotspots. A successful crappie angler will have the desire and determination to learn how to analyze a lake to find the productive fishing areas. Reading informative articles and books, studying maps and then getting out on the water with a game plan and appropriate maps are keys to success. Knowing what to do under certain conditions to locate and catch crappie will some day be rewarding. Putting facts to use at the right time is what takes fish and makes good fishermen.

In most bodies of water, crappie schools move about. They may be relatively easy to locate in the spring when they move shallow to spawn, but the rest of the year, they can be difficult to find. The often-nomadic crappie do, however, tend to move in relation to certain things or hold on certain structures, like the submerged auto. Underwater creek channels, vegetation, timber, points and other structure may be magnets to the fish.

Mapping Pointers

One of the keys to analyzing a lake is to be familiar with a good topographical map which shows tributary channels, depths and other bottom characteristics. The very best maps also have additional information such as soil materials, water clarity and fertility, inlets and thermocline information. I helped produce maps with such information for several lakes in Florida. The "Map and Research Reports" include fishery survey information, forage base, fish migration patterns and much more.

The maps also include detailed Lake Survey information regarding the best areas to fish for the different species of fish present. The maps are waterproof, tearproof and they even float. If you can find one for the lake you fish, get it.

Successful crappie fishing strategies can be determined from good topographical maps, if you know what to look for. Research, before you go to the lake, will help minimize the travel on-the-water. Developing productive patterns quickly after the launch may depend on your ability to interpret topo lines.

Successful crappie fishing strategies can be determined from good topographical maps, if you know what to look for. Research, before you go to the lake, will help minimize the travel on-the-water. Developing productive, crappie-catching patterns quickly on unfamiliar waters depends on your ability to interpret topo lines.

"The closest contour lines will be the sharpest drop points and the areas that fish usually relate to," a mapmaker once told me. "When you have a good idea of the depth and type of water the crappie are holding in, you can develop a good pattern using a topo map."

103

Flat pad areas can be productive in the spring. Maps with contour lines greatly separated could denote spawning flats. The good maps will reveal little ditches or ridges in the flat areas and there might be massive numbers of fish concentrated there.

"It doesn't have to be a great depth change, just anywhere those contour lines come together and provide a change - at the back of a pocket, or out on a point," he explained. "Even the smallest amount of change, like from three to six feet, if it's a sharp drop, may hold concentrations of crappie."

Channels And Points

Most successful anglers will check out the points with submerged channels nearby. That's usually where structure will exist on the bottom. When the lake bottom was cleared prior to impoundment, the cutters avoid areas hard to get to, or they just cut off trees as they can reach them leaving stumps. Crappie relate to such changes. On roadbeds, points, underwater bridges, fence lines, or old tree rows, crappie will relate to the change in the bottom, wherever the sharpest dropoff occurs.

There might be a road ditch paralleling the treeline and an old creek crossing the ditch; usually that type of area is the place you are looking for on topo maps. A good topo map will also show you the coves and creeks that have definite channels, which is very important in the springtime when you're looking for concentrations of spawning crappie. A flat cove or pocket without a channel in it will have very few fish, normally.

Flat areas can be good in the spring, though. Areas with lines that are greatly separated are spawning flats. The good maps will reveal little ditches or ridges in the flat areas and there might be massive numbers of fish concentrated in one area. A large flat area that makes for a good spawning ground may have a ditch or channel that leads to outside drops or channels nearby, and even more schools of crappie may be concentrated in such an area.

Topo Maps

So, depending on the time of year, you have an idea what to look for on a topo map. Try to dissect the map. For example, deeper water just off the flats could be a good post-spawn or early-spawn area. In early spring, crappie often bunch up off points and over humps. When they're in the shallows, they'll be more scattered out, but on a point they'll be bunched, and that's another thing to look for.

If a channel comes nearby, crappie schools may use that for summertime activity. The bends in a deep channel are always good. The outside bends are slightly higher than the inside bends, and usually they'll have more brush on them.

One doesn't have to slip on SCUBA gear to find crappie... only learn how they relate to the structure that lies below. Through topo maps and electronics, a smart angler will catch more crappie.

Chapter 17

ELECTRONICS STRATEGIES

A depth finder comes in handy to verify the information found on any topographical map. Crappie schools will move up or down a channel until they find the kind of water that's good for them. The best areas will usually have a combination of underwater structure, deep water and flats. With the LCD, flasher or chart recorder, check out little areas that appear different from others.

Once you have selected the general areas that look good on a topo map, use the sonar unit on the water to quickly check out the spots. There could very well be something on the map that doesn't show, like a little ditch that cuts across a point. The school of crappie could be stacked in that depression.

Once you get on a lake and develop a productive pattern, such as ''crappie in 15 feet of water and positioned over a sharp break'', you can pull out the map and follow the 15-foot contour line until it comes closest to a 30-foot contour line, for example. That will be a sharp, vertical drop from the crest of 15-foot water and a good area!

Most bodies of water have several excellent types of crappie structure that can be found with the aid of sonar. On my chart recorder, I've even discovered sunken boats, and such structure almost always holds crappie. Never overlook a sunken object. Crappie prefer cover such as submerged vegetation, brush piles,

107

rock formations and other "below-water markings" noted on the electronics.

Emergent structures, such as pilings, piers and docks, are scattered throughout many lakes, and they can be a gold mine. Crappie relate to man-made cover just like any other fresh or saltwater fish does. Some of my largest and best stringers of crappie were taken off deep wood structure in Florida's Crescent Lake. Great stringers of crappie also came from a near a dock in 15 feet of water on a sandpit in central Kansas.

Schools of crappie usually prefer deeper water with some form of structure when available. While some fishermen have caught large non-spawning crappie in the shallows, most of the "slabs" prefer to be in the depths. For them, safety and protection lies in deep water; they spend most of their time there.

Electronic Color Selections

Once you have located a concentration of crappie with the sonar unit, lure color is an important factor that can cause a strike. The fish's color preference may be based on biological, environmental or other reasons difficult to define. Angler experience, however, has resulted in some conclusions on lure color selection. Certain lure colors seem to correlate with a type of strike behavior, which makes them very effective.

According to Dick Healey of Lake Systems Division, manufacturer of the Color-C-Lector, an "aggravating type" lure such as a small spinnerbait may be most productive when sporting fluorescent, red or yellow colors. Correspondingly, a food source imitator may be most productive in muted, forage colors. The tiny soft plastics, like the Berkley Power Grubs, generally move slower through the depths or near the bottom and are good examples of such.

Similarly, a small vibrating shad plug like the 1/8 ounce Bill Lewis Tiny Trap, imitates little shad, and silver with black or blue back is often the most effective hue to fish in open waters. In the springtime, most southern lakes have schools of tiny shad that move about in open waters feeding on algae plankton near

Once you have selected the general areas that look good on a topo map, use the sonar unit on the water to quickly check out the spots. There could very well be something on the map that doesn't show, like a little ditch that cuts across a point. The school of crappie could be stacked in that depression.

the surface. You can often see the schools on the sonar unit, and then, artificials that resemble the shad should be productive in those spots.

For most of us, our lure color choice is based on such factors as cloud cover, water clarity, angle of the sun and water depth. Often, the chosen weapon works, but just as often, educated guesses are wrong, and crappie are not to be found. Weather, which influences the mood of fish, also may play a role in determining the optimal color of lure to toss, according to Healey. Inactive fish in a passive state may be enticed by more subdued, dark colors.

109

The best areas will usually have a combination of underwater structure, deep water and flats. With the LCD, flasher or chart recorder, check out little areas that appear different from others.

"More aggressive fish may be interested in brighter lure color combinations and choices," points out Healey. "A school of crappie moving through an area with abundant forage may, in fact, go after a bright, chartreuse jig or small plug."

For those wanting some assistance in determining the best color to use under given conditions such as clarity and light penetration, Lake Systems Division (Rt. 3, Box 233-M, Mt. Vernon, MO 65712) has an instrument called, the Color-C-Lector. By dropping the light meter probe into the water at any depth, a percent light transmittance value will appear, and that is correlated to the color most visible to fish under the particular water clarity, time of day, and sky condition. The instrument is available at most tackle stores and sporting goods.

Loran and GPS Technology

Knowing the longitude and latitude of productive fishing areas may not be an important aspect of crappie fishing, but the technology associated with these terms could prove to be invaluable on large reservoirs and natural lakes. This technology is becoming more and more popular with multi-species anglers, especially since its application does not depend on specific fish types.

The Loran C (and more recently Global Positioning Systems or GPS) navigational system has long been used by saltwater fishing guides to mark and relocate productive fishing spots. Because it was initially developed for saltwater, it has taken the freshwater angling community a long time to realize it offers some important benefits for inland waters. On big waters where the schools of crappie may be one or two miles off shore or the nearest weedline, this technology is important.

The Loran and GPS units are small devices which gather longitude and latitude signals that are transmitted from various sources throughout the country and skies (satellites). When a 'honey hole' has been located, the positioning unit reads the longitude and latitude of that location and the data is programmed into the unit. The exact spot can be easily found hours, days or weeks later. The unit also details the distance and the amount of time needed to arrive at the location from your favorite launch ramp or marina. The units are expensive but they could have an application on your lake!

Talking to successful fishermen and local guides about a particular lake is one way to establish a game plan of action. They are often willing to share information and make analyzing the waters easier. Once you have information about an effective pattern (depth, structure and lure), you can go to your topo map and electronics to capitalize on it. Then, knowing how fish behavior and habitat interplay will enable you to catch a bunch of crappie.

Chapter 18

THE CRAPPIE pHISHING CONCEPT

Bill Dance, popular TV show host and professional fisherman, built his reputation on bass fishing, but the Tennessee native is also an accomplished crappie angler. So is Dr. Loren Hill, inventor of the Color-C-Lector and the pH Guide.

When the pH Guide first hit the market several years ago, Dance invited Dr. Hill to join him on Sardis Reservoir for some speck action. The obvious intent was to verify the accuracy of the new instrument and learn a little more about its limitations and operation.

Dance didn't know how effective the pH Guide would be when he met Hill that day. He was eager to find out, though. The pH system would work for crappie, Dr. Hill contended. They jumped in Dance's boat and took off in search of elusive specks.

They initially pulled up to a long tree line that jutted into the lake. They took pH readings at increments of one foot from the surface all the way to the 18-foot bottom. The biggest change occurred at 9 feet. There the pH went from 7.8 to 7.6.

The two respected anglers decided to experiment and test the concept by fishing different depths. After one hour of fishing at the 6-foot depth, Dance had the only strike. Both Dance and Dr. Hill then tried the 9 foot depth and began to catch huge crappie immediately.

113

They were pulling in their eleventh large crappie when an old man, recognizing Dance, came closer in his small boat. Dance asked him if he had caught anything and the man answered that he had a "box full".

Dance asked him to pull over alongside of the boat so he could take the old fellow's picture. Dr. Hill had never seen such big crappie in his life! When asked what depth he was fishing, the man answered "nine feet"!

The older gentleman didn't have a pH Guide to tell him the right depth, but Dr. Hill and Dance had put the instrument and concept to the test. It had predicted the specks to be most active at nine feet. That is where the fish were caught on that particular day.

All you need to do is to ask some very basic questions and allow the water you are fishing to provide the answers. That's what Dr. Hill, director of biological research at the University of Oklahoma, says.

According Hill, the pH method is the most useful and reliable technique anyone can use in establishing the correct pattern and depth for catching crappie or any other species of fish. It works in any body of water in any part of the country. The university professor has experimented with water chemistry for several years while developing the method.

"pH is simply the most valuable tool we know for fishermen," he says. "And it applies to all fish species, including crappie."

The pH method for fishing is based upon two considerations:

1) observing the pH on the surface of the water, and

2) checking pH at each foot below the surface to the bottom. Using a pH meter is relatively easy.

The Method

Once on the water, turn on the pH monitor and simply read the surface pH in the area of the lake you plan to fish. Do not go to the lake looking for a specific or exact pH because fish must live with the environmental conditions that exist or occur within that lake!

114

All species of fish are very aggressive and easy to catch when the pH is between about 7.2 and 8.8. For crappie, the ideal range is 7.2 to 7.4. When the pH is above 8.0 or below 7.0, specks become less aggressive and more difficult to catch.

All species of fish are very aggressive and easy to catch when the pH is between about 7.2 and 8.8. For crappie, the ideal range is 7.2 to 7.4. When the pH is above 8.0 or below 7.0, specks become less aggressive and more difficult to catch. If you find certain sections of the lake that are below pH 7.0, you are going to have some trouble catching them in those areas because they are stressed,

If you find that the entire lake has a pH below 7.0 on the surface, look for the highest pH you can find, for example, pH 6.3, and fish your lures slower. If the surface pH is continually above 8.0, you should not necessarily avoid these areas. The pH will change with depth and will almost always be lower several feet below the surface. Thus, the fish will probably be caught below the surface at a depth where the pH drops.

Once you have determined the pH on the surface, the next step is to determine what depth you should be fishing by using the pH Guide, which has a weighted probe. Drop the probe below the surface and read the pH at each foot to the bottom. Wherever you

115

see the biggest change between one foot to the next is called the pH breakline. The crappie will normally be stacked at or extremely near this depth!

After you have found the breakline, which may be as small as two-tenths of a unit (7.3 to 7.1), you know you should not be fishing any deeper. If, for example, you find the biggest change occurs between 7 and 8 feet deep, then you know you can catch fish from the surface down to 8 feet deep. However, most of the crappie will be as close to the 8-foot breakline as they can, and possibly be associated with structure.

Once you're aware of the pH on the surface and have also determined the pH breakline at the correct depth, you can immediately establish your fishing pattern to keep you in the right areas and proper depth to catch fish.

For example, if you found that the surface pH ranged from 6.7 in one area to 7.8 in another, with most of the lake giving a pH reading of 7.5 on the surface, you should immediately concentrate your fishing in areas with a pH above 7.0 on the surface. If you then found the pH breakline to be at five feet, you could position your boat in open water and work structure at five feet (for example, standing timber or telephone poles) over 20 to 30 feet of water.

If you are trolling for specks, position the lures approximately one to two feet above the breakline. You may use a downrigger or select a lure that can be trolled at a known depth close to the pH breakline.

If you are cane pole fishing for crappie, check the pH breakline and set the length of your line so your bait is suspended about one foot above the breakline. While some fish can be caught below the pH breakline in deeper water, your success will be much greater above the breakline.

"During the past couple of years, I have experienced some fantastic conditions with pH and fishing all over the country," says Dr. Hill. "The pH system for crappie fishing has been tremendous in all kinds of different conditions and in different states."

pH levels can be influenced by springs, chemical pollutants, soil type of lake bottom and surface runoff from adjoining fields. Submerged trees and fallen brush can likewise lower or raise the values in their vicinity, depending upon the variety.

The Research

The technique of utilizing pH level meters to find fish has been around since Dr. Hill studied relations between water quality and fish behavior in the early 1970's. His studies revealed that crappie have a marked preference for a specific pH.

117

That preference, he found, is to a large degree physical, i.e., based on internal requirements related to the pH of the crappie's body fluids.

Dr. Hill's experiments revealed that fish require a balance between the pH of their blood and that of their body fluids. He discovered that most fishes blood, including crappie, is slightly alkaline, so it was not surprising that they seek water with approximately the same pH.

Another finding was that water with extreme pH levels are generally void of fish. While fish can stand levels that range across three rating points, their preference may vary only 0.2 to 0.5 on the pH scale. Further studies have shown that pH is more important than water temperature and dissolved oxygen concentration.

All liquids vary in pH and bodies of water do also, from area to area. In the same way that we measure hot and cold in units of temperature, we can measure acid and alkaline in units of pH. The lowest reading on the scale (0.0) is the strongest acid and the highest reading (14.0) is the strongest alkaline. "Pure", distilled water has a pH of 7.0.

Weather and Other Influences

In colder climates, the pH of entire lakes become very nearly the same in the winter months. This is due to the reduced influence of streams, to slower plant life decomposition, and to the absence of photosynthesis in green plants. In general, though, the surface pH is normally the highest and the bottom pH is the lowest.

The winter pH of most lakes will be between 6.0 and 7.5, but acid rain, snow or ice can draw pH much lower. While pH is falling slowly through fall and early winter, fish are continually re-acclimating to it, usually with no obvious behavior changes. However, their behavior does change gradually, because as pH drops, their rate of efficiency in utilizing oxygen drops also.

In the early spring (February in the South), plant growth causes pH to rise. It is then during spawning that pH values are especially critical, according to Joe Meirick, manufacturer of pH

Guide. His Lake Systems Division, which has been producing the Guide for years, introduced an additional pH instrument with increased capabilities, the Combo-C-Lector. The Combo unit will tell you the temperature of the water and lure color to use.

Dr. Hill recommends that you think of the pH instruments as time saving devices, since you can use them to cull large areas that would be time consuming to fish thoroughly. Find water with the right pH range and you'll have a good chance of finding a few (or more) crappie.

Other influences of pH levels include springs, chemical pollutants, bottom soil type and surface runoff from adjoining fields. Submerged trees and fallen brush can likewise lower or raise the values, depending upon the variety. This condition is often found in newly inundated impoundments or in areas that are easily affected by storms.

Acid rain has been found to be as low as 1.7 pH in parts of the country and an influx can alter any water. The pH of clean rain is approximately 5.6, so even heavy amounts of it can lower the pH of a body of water. The weak acid introduced through rainfall affects pH of the surface and near-surface waters primarily. If a strong wind exists, however, the mixing action can change pH levels throughout the lake.

pH levels not only impact crappie but also their forage. Zoo-plankton, microscopic animal organisms, live in colonies that feed on phyto-plankton and require pH values below 8.5 to live. Tiny shad prefer a pH range of 8.4 to 8.8, crayfish between 7.3 and 7.8, and shiner minnows 7.9 to 8.4. Small bluegill, a favorite crappie prey, prefer a pH range of 7.7 to 7.9. As with any species find the forage, find the predator.

The pH method for fishing is a simple, yet deadly, method that any fisherman can use. Just go to the lake without any pre-determined ideas, ask some very basic questions. The lake has all the answers!

119

Chapter 19

MARK YOUR HONEY HOLES

A cloud of fish seemed to hover over the submerged tree, according to my chart recorder. I slowly moved past the structure as my partner slipped a yellow marker buoy over the side. The fish were about 15 feet below the surface in the top of the small tree, so I figured they wouldn't spook.

Our first casts confirmed that. Two crappie, each about a pound in weight, grabbed the bucktail jigs. We landed them, and cast again near the marker. Our jigs were in a free-fall when I noticed my 6-pound test line twitch again. The light spinning rod bowed sharply as I set the hook. I quickly put the crappie in the boat, and turned to notice my partner sweeping his rod back.

His fish pulled off, but we continued to catch crappie. Sometimes, we would catch three fish on three casts, other times we would make five to 10 casts before a strike. Often, we had doubles. We caught 30 some crappie from that one spot before the remaining fish lost interest.

We had discovered the spot in the middle of the lake by following a creek channel out of a cove. Without the aid of our sonar and, ultimately, the marker buoy, we certainly wouldn't have amassed such a livewell full of crappie. The flatlands reservoir had very little in the way of landmarks to line up on. Trying to keep the boat positioned about 30 feet off the crappie-laden structure by sonar alone would have been almost impossible.

121

A marker was the only way to effectively hone in on the "honey hole."

The most important aspect of successful crappie fishing is, accordingly, locating the fish. Most anglers can catch them once they are near a concentration. That is usually the easy part.

Finding crappie is part of the picture and marking their location in order to make the most effective presentation is a component of successfully fishing a school. Another important part of the picture, especially if you are going to return the following day, is finding the great spot once again.

To a fisherman who chases schools of crappie or other panfish, the use of markers, either buoys or natural, is often valuable. Knowing how to use both types is what often separates the successful anglers from the novices.

Man-made Buoys

Guides and other avid fishermen often place marker buoys to establish the exact location of a crappie concentration. If a crappie angler is trolling and catches a fish, he should immediately throw a buoy out to mark the place where he caught that fish. Then, he should concentrate on fishing that area. Crappie are schooling fish, and they are seldom by themselves.

As soon as a concentration of fish is located, the angler should throw another buoy overboard on the upwind or shallow side. Then, he should immediately swing the boat back toward deeper water, dropping back downwind away from the fish concentration. The final movement is to come back toward the fish from downwind or deep water and throw out another buoy to mark the range of the concentration. Then, casts between the two buoys should result in strikes.

If the outboard motor is running, it is smart to simply place one buoy on the school, shut off the engine and fish the area with the trolling motor until another fish is caught. Then, toss another buoy to further define the position of the school. If you locate a concentration of crappie, you can often drop a buoy and come back 20 minutes later to fish it more effectively.

Most successful anglers prefer to use natural markers when they can. Natural markers usually mean a tree or treeline out in the lake. Shoreline markers can be docks, trees, homes, a number of things, but make sure that whatever you use for a marker is a permanent one.

When you toss the buoy out, place it on the other side of the boat, not on top of where you caught the fish. The unwinding buoy won't scare the others awaiting their "forage" to swim by. Another way of marking a piece of physical structure that holds fish is to drop the buoy where the boat should be positioned to catch the fish. That will help you position the boat accurately, so that you can more effectively fish the key spot and not have to worry about a fish getting tangled up in the line. You don't want the buoy sitting right on top of the structure or school, because a hooked fish might get fouled in it. You then could lose the crappie or the fish could 'unmark' the place. It's best to line up the structure being fished with a landmark so that you can cast accurately to the fish.

It is difficult to use marker buoys when there are numerous other boats on the water searching for the same fish. Some guides will use their trolling motor to set out the marker buoy, and then fish the area until they determine exactly how the school is positioned. Then, they will use a natural marker and note the depth.

Natural Markers

If the area looks like it is a permanent seasonal attraction to a school of crappie, and you want to come back later to fish it, use natural markers. Line up two trees, a house, a boat dock or about anything along the shoreline. If you don't have a reference point, you can lose your location very quickly in open water and not catch as many fish as you should.

You'll have to line up two definite marks, but this is an especially good way to mark a treetop, ledge or hump where you have caught several fish and want to leave it to return later without having additional boats on the spot. Generally, you will want to establish a specific depth and try to stay at that depth until you reach the ledge and can follow it with your trolling motor.

Most successful anglers prefer to use natural markers when they can. Natural markers usually mean a tree or treeline out in the lake. Shoreline markers can be docks, trees, homes, a number of things, but make sure that whatever you use for a marker is a permanent one. Always a good natural marker, gaps in the treeline usually don't change overnight. You can often use this type of marker at night also. Fishing submerged structure in the middle of a lake is relatively easy by using the gaps in a treeline.

Most anglers use something on the shoreline like a clump of grass as a reference point. If you're fishing deep water, 20 to 25 feet, and there is a lot of standing timber, you can use the emergent trees or stumps projecting above the water's surface for markers. You can relate your distance from them when you locate a school of fish. Use the depth finder to determine the depth of water and then refer to the relative position from the emergent stump. You can then mark your position without having to put a marker buoy out.

You have to make mental notes when using natural markers just to keep casting at the exact area. If you don't pay attention to the shoreline markers, you'll find yourself unsure that you are on the spot where you initially caught the fish. When you are two or three miles from shore fishing in open water and the lake depth is pretty much the same, you may not even have reference points. There's really no way to mark the location by water depth and natural markers, so you have to use buoys.

Triangulation is a good way to mark a hot spot. You'll need three points to visually mark a spot. For example, line up a couple of trees on one bank and a third point on another to triangulate the spot. You'll also need to keep a pen and notebook in the boat and handy to write the location down. Draw a triangle to find your way back to the particular spot.

Keep in mind that your emergent structure reference point might change - somebody could cut the tree down. Keep that in mind too when on shallow waters, where reed or other tall emergent vegetation patches all look alike. On hard to find spots, it's a good idea to have backup markers, just in case something changes. Write these down, and don't simply trust them to memory.

No matter what you use, try to triangulate the spot to make it easy and precise to find. In rivers, the channel buoy markers can be great to line up on, but be aware that they can change from season to season.

Keeping The Hole Secret

If you try to locate areas out of the main natural flow of boat traffic, you have a better chance of keeping the spot to yourself. If you find a concentration of fish in the flow of traffic and want to go back to them the next day, a combination natural/buoy system may be most suited. The "buoy" should be a small, inconspicuous marker. If you know the general vicinity, you can pull right up to the buoy. If not, you'll generally use a shoreline mark to get you in the general area, and then find the smaller object that has been placed there.

Some guides who want to keep their honey holes productive and secret for a long time will even go pretty far in covering up their location. One told me that he used an aspirin bottle with a 1/2 ounce slip sinker tied on 10 lb test line to mark a piece of structure that always held a concentration of fish. He fished the spot several days and almost always caught a bunch of crappie.

125

To position his unusual marker, he backed the boat off the honey hole about 25 feet and dropped the aspirin bottle. Then, when he returned, he would position his boat on the aspirin bottle and have his clients throw to where he knew the crappie were concentrated. Such markers are not very obvious to other fishermen. You can't see an aspirin bottle very easily, but using bright colored marker buoys will attract a lot more attention and company!

Some crappie guides have marked their top-producing brush piles with small pieces of styrofoam or cork tied to a length of monofilament. Such markers are tough for passing boats to spot, but they can save the guide a lot of time when he needs to produce fish fast. To position the styrofoam piece precisely, you need to know exactly how deep the water is. Then, you can adjust the length of line so that the heavy weight pulls the styrofoam down three or four inches below the surface of the water. That makes the marker even harder for someone else to find.

Another approach to take is to use something that floats naturally, like a little stick. It would not be unusual to see a piece of wood floating in the water. Simply tie a light piece of monofilament, six or eight pound test, to it, and a big sinker to complete the ''natural'' marker.

Make Your Own or Buy Them

To make your own buoys, simply find a piece of strong, closed-cell styrofoam block. Take a knife and carefully notch out part of the middle section to form a crude ''barbell'' of sorts. Each end should be flat, if possible, to prevent the line from continuing to roll off the buoy after the weight has reached the bottom.

Once the shape is perfected, then tie a 50 foot piece of nylon cord to the mid-section and wrap the line on. Use a one ounce sinker or lead weight as an anchor, and you are in business. Small plastic jugs or bottles may suffice, but keeping the cord wound tightly on them can be a problem.

The alternative, of course, is to purchase your own. They are sold by marine dealers, tackle stores and mail order catalog houses. Most retail for about three to five dollars each and come with 60 to 75 yards of cord and lead weights. The markers are usually bright orange or yellow in color and constructed of high-impact styrene or polyethylene plastic.

A marker buoy is a great memory system for fishermen. Coupled with electronics, it allows anglers after concentrations of crappie, panfish or other schooling species that relate to structure, to maximize their catch.

Crappie Tactics

128

Chapter 20

MAKING SENSE OF SCENT PRODUCTS

Scent products are becoming more of a force in the industry because they work. Manufacturers have focused on developing attractants for crappie fishermen, and tackle store shelves are stocked fully. Research backing up manufacturers' claims of the importance of scent products is available now, and the attractant industry is advancing rapidly.

Manufacturers claim that their products work on inactive fish, those not actively feeding. Active crappie will hit just about any small lure or bait, and the difference between consistently catching large numbers or a few is in attracting the inactive fish. Crappie, like other types of fish, rely primarily on five senses to survive from day to day. The sense of smell and taste play a particularly important role in their behavior.

In waters with limited visibility, smell and taste are particularly well-developed in fish. Crappie will usually take their time in analyzing the smell of a lure or bait, therefore, fishing scented artificials slower than one normally would is advisable. An inactive fish, given time to discern the scent, may decide to feed on the lure or bait. Optimal conditions for using a scent product, many say, may be in cold water when most fish rely more on their sense of smell, after cold fronts when fish are

129

seldom aggressively chasing lures, and on slow-moving lure fishing.

Regardless of when you decide to apply some attractant, it's quite possible that you may catch larger fish. Research has shown that crappie and most other species of fish appear to develop a more defined olfactory system as they grow. That's important to those seeking larger fish.

Fish apparently can recognize their own kind by a particular smell, and in fact, they can even communicate with one another through "chemical communication." According to biologists, each fish has a distinctive body odor. Tests have shown that laboratory specimens of some minnows have been trained to distinguish the odors of over a dozen different species of fish. Thus, they may be able to differentiate between which fish to "hang out" with and which not to.

A school of minnows may be driven literally up a wall or bank by the smell of a school of crappie, according to researchers. An alarm substance is released by some forage species when danger threatens. Injured baitfish often have a traumatic effect on the remainder of the school. They seemingly cause the school to reel in fright. Since each species of preyfish is made up of differing proportions of amino acids, the building blocks of all protein (and flesh), a scent product comprised of the right combination of amino acids could be attractive to crappie.

Scents Attract Anglers

Many fish scents have shown that they can attract fishermen. Annual sales are in the neighborhood of $50 million, and over 50 makers of scent products reportedly exist. Several manufacturers have testimonials from biologists, weekend fishermen and professional anglers alike that their offering is productive. A few companies like Berkley have a staff of scientists researching and testing products on fish in the laboratory. In fact, Berkley invested thousands of hours in the initial development of their attractant.

Fish use their sense of smell to detect food and danger. Crappie sniff out their prey, according to scientific studies. That's why live grass shrimp taken right from their feeding flats can be an effective bait.

Scent product manufacturers spend a lot of time in the lab developing ways to make their formulas productive and "fishable." One problem that several have overcome is that scent molecules are sometimes slow to permeate the water, yet they can be carried off quickly by current. That's usually a trade-off each producer has to consider.

Oil-based fish scents wash off a lure and float to the surface while those that are "water soluble" mix with the surrounding water to create a potent smell path. That "strategic dispersion" can be detectable in minute concentrations, according to the lab boys.

The slower the presentation, the more important smell and use of scent products become. Since faster retrieves don't rely on the fish's sense of smell as much for enticement, most scent fishermen use the slower baits and presentations. That will give the fish more time to detect the favorable odors given off as the lure is retrieved.

131

Attractants are usually more beneficial on inactive fish or those under heavy fishing pressure. They will become increasingly important when the conditions are tough, when few are able to successfully pattern the fish. Obviously, when the fish are hitting most everything thrown at them, the addition of an attractant makes little sense. Not many days are like that though.

Soft baits

Soft baits normally take a scent and retain it better than hard lures. For example, attractants adhere better to plastic grubs, jigs and small spinnerbait skirts. Most scent products don't last long when applied to slick finishes, like a tiny crankbait.

Attractants may make the artificial more "natural" to the predator fish through their smelling sense. Certainly a fish will reach a point of go or no-go as it approaches a lure and the scent may then make the difference in the final decision. It could trigger the response that all anglers hope for - the strike.

To trigger a "go" decision, some attractants disperse tiny scales or oil bubbles, both visual attractants of sorts. Others are slow to "dissolve" and make claims of lasting longer. The time between applications depends on which product you are using and to whom you are talking. Most of the scents on the market today last anywhere from "five casts to 30 minutes", depending on the lure and retrieve.

Not all scent products are developed as purely attractants; a few also mask smells that can be potential "turn-offs". Their use tends to camouflage any smell transferred to the lure or bait from handling or other means. Odors from gasoline, insect repellent, reel oil, and human sweat should be masked, according to many researchers.

Unfavorable odors turn fish off. According to test results from experiments conducted at Berkley's Fish Research Center, one of the most repulsive chemicals to fish is insect repellent. Most of us use a sunscreen when on the water these days, and many of them can also be offensive to fish. Anglers should try to be extremely careful to keep all unfavorable-type odors off his hands and fishing tackle.

Fish Scent Dispersion Patterns

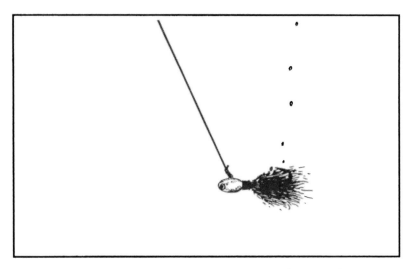

Fish can smell and taste. Fish attractants dissolve into the water in a time-controlled manner. Oil-based formulas (above) float to the surface, while water-based formulas (below) mixes with water for a "time controlled" release.

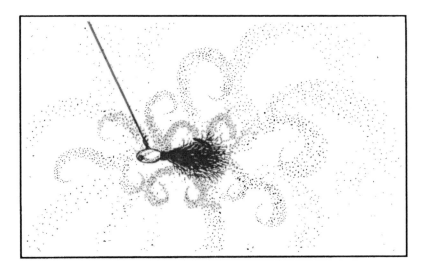

133

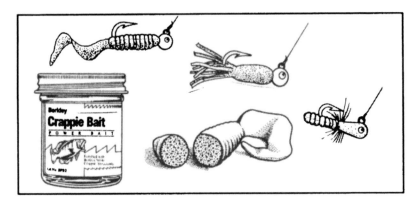

Product Research

Good scent products line the shelves of most tackle shops, and Berkley has more than their share of space. Probably no other manufacturer has committed as much research to a complete scent product line. Their scientists have spent years in underwater and laboratory research on man's ability to influence fish behavior.

Some of the better products comes in water-soluble liquid or solid, moldable form for strategic dispersion and are designed to appeal to the chemoreception senses. The time-controlled release insures a more lengthy effectiveness. The liquid form of some attractants is bottled in convenient containers.

Berkley's Power Bait is a jar-contained, Strike-type attractant in specie-specific formulations for panfish. The white bait has a long-lasting, milking action that disperses scent. Power Baits are true baits and not additive products, although they may be used that way at times. From Bass Buster's ''Candy Counter'' comes Crappie Candy, a bait formulated from natural foods. It is available in three colors. Several other manufacturers also offer crappie attractants in one form or another.

The sense of smell of most sport fish is used to detect food and danger. Crappie aren't usually considered to be fish that sniff out their prey, but scientific studies have revealed that their noses are more important to them than originally thought. Sense of smell plays a larger role in their daily lives than most anglers realize. As a result, scent products are here to stay.

Chapter 21

CATCH TIDEWATER CRAPPIE

We had only been on the water about two hours and were casting small spinners to a fresh water cut from the river toward the salty East Bay when we heard two outboard motors start up just ahead of us. Soon the two boats rounded the bend, heading for us until one of them moved ahead and across the small creek stretching a net taut between them. The water lying ahead of us was muddied for at least half a mile and our fishing for the morning was, in effect, shot.

The four weekend fishermen were haul netting for salt water fish, but I wonder how many crappie, bluegill and bass are killed by their technique. This 'sport' is legal in some tidal-influenced areas and unfortunately, those areas encompass several miles of superb fresh water crappie fishing. Many coastal estuaries may be unpolluted, but instances such as the this endanger this condition.

The coastal estuary is a different 'breed of cat' which may be unfamiliar to many freshwater anglers. It is a unique blend of rivers, creeks, freshwater and brackish marshes, wooded and shrub swamps and in some cases, even bays.

Vast tidal river systems puncture the Gulf Coast and the lower east coast and most contain crappie fishing. Literally thousands of miles of brackish water exist along the U.S. coastline from Texas to Maryland.

Most of the coastal state's fish and game departments have limited knowledge of the tidal-influenced freshwater fishery. While the marine fisheries biologists are conducting various programs and studies on saltwater life in the estuaries, the fresh water boys have little to do with brackish water studies on their respective fishery. Consequently, this is an area which needs further study and development of sound knowledge.

Most of the productive crappie anglers on the coast are very tight-lipped about the action and want little notoriety for their favorite honey holes. After all, word of their success could spread, bringing more people and, in some cases, more pollution.

Pollution, in whatever form, has a devastating effect on the delicately-balanced tidal ecosystem. The effect of this and other influences on the coastal estuaries determine the level of crappie fishing productivity to be found.

Many of the productive crappie fisheries near the coasts lie in unique biological and ecological estuaries. Many are relatively shallow; many have some sort of island barriers to the sea and most are high density areas for fish, wildlife and plants. The types of floodplain forests and swamps usually encountered in such areas support important habitats to both saltwater and freshwater fish.

Salinity Distribution

Many brackish waters lie in a relatively natural state, which contributes to the high numbers of crappie found in such environments. Crappie in this ecosystem are dominated by the salinity distribution, nutrients present and fluctuations of the tributaries. These drainage characteristics are most important to a prosperous fishery.

Ecological systems in coastal drainage basins have been said to be in states of 'dynamic equilibrium.' What happens at one part will, in some way, affect the other parts. Too high a salinity

Forage can be affected easier (at times) than the crappie, and a lack of small crustacean and minnows that are staples in a brackish water crappie diet may lead to slow starvation. The effect on any part of the food chain can have a profound effect on the crappie. This crappie tried to gulp down a small bluegill!

content in the bays and swamps may cause the crappie to move upstream to narrow river tributaries which drain higher lands.

Crappie are moved about considerably in the coastal estuaries by the water character. Man's involvement in damming, dredging and polluting tidal-influenced waters can definitely change the quality of an ecosystem. The effects of pollution, reduced nutrients and increased salinity have caused many coastal crappie death at a young age.

Forage can be affected easier (at times) than the crappie, and a lack of small crustacean and minnows that are staples in a brackish water crappie diet may lead to slow starvation. The effect on any part of the food chain can have a profound effect on the crappie.

The more river-influenced the estuary, the more likely it is to be crappie water. Rivers bring in both dissolved nutrients, such as nitrates and phosphates, and other organic matter such as leaves, branches, etc., from upstream. In addition to the important upland areas, an estuary full of small microscopic plants (phytoplankton) can be a prolific environment for crappie forage.

Phytoplankton productivity, low salinity and nutrient rich waters depend on the flow rate and fluctuations of the tributaries. Wetlands with some annual flooding appear to be conducive to a crappie fishery. Leaf matter and small forage are swept downriver during high water periods and brackish waters are 'freshened' up.

Swift currents and high turbidity result in temporarily poor angling, but the overall effect of water level changes in the estuary is important. It is a rejuvenation of sorts to the entire coastal ecosystem and something that is imperative to the fresh water crappie fishing in such an area.

Crappie forage also depends on natural cycles of the waterways and a lack of flushing action affects all predator. Silting can destroy important brackish water habitat for snails, clams, crabs and other shellfish.

The spawn of fish which live in fresh or brackish water and migrate to saltwater in order to spawn can be an important forage for crappie. Eels and mullet are two such fish, and the coastal crappie definitely likes to eat the young of both. Other tiny fingerlings of coastal water fish such as flounder, redfish and sea trout also become part of the food chain.

Salty Predators
The predators of brackish water crappie are often a major concern. Marine species such as black drum, redfish and stripers grow to large sizes and all eat their share of crappie and other fish. Alligators, furry varmints and large birds are also abundant in the tidal marshes and coastal estuaries, and many of them are proficient at foraging on unwary crappie.

Man's effect on the estuary has been felt in all areas of the country. We have dammed, diked, filled and dredged coastal waters and many times, problems have arisen.

Tributaries have been dredged for barge traffic, and the spoil from the channels disposed of on nearby banks. Dredging causes a shifting of sediments and destroys organisms in the food chain. Disposal of the dredged material destroys vegetation and is

Many brackish water estuaries have very short tributaries and the drainage consists primarily of low marsh lands. Many tidal-influenced rivers are stained mahogany by the tannic acid from cypress, mangrove and other swamp vegetation. Water from sawgrass marshes with few trees generally is not quite as dark, however.

detrimental to the flood plain and river. Silt can smother tree roots and plants, reducing needed cover in the estuary.

Rivers and tributaries with barge traffic are de-snagged, which also has an impact on the fishery. Removing snags from the water reduces valuable cover for the crappie and shelter for its forage. Reduction of habitat here has the same effect on crappie fishing as it would in a freshwater lake.

The damming of a tidal-influenced tributary has many effects on crappie angling. Dams block the migration of even the smallest eels, shad, striped bass and other fish, many of which provide forage for crappie. The flow of nutrients may also be reduced, which can hurt the fish food organism production in the estuary.

Dams can limit the flow of freshwater and stop saltwater intrusion, making any tidal influenced action below it strictly for marine saltwater species. Dams are also used to maintain deeper channels, which tend to decrease the oxygen content in those areas of reduced flow velocity. During low water, the Trinity and San Jacinto Rivers in Texas are particularly susceptible to low oxygen content. They turn into 'catfish waters' in these hard times.

Industrial pollution also may have an adverse impact on the coastal crappie fishing. Commercial barge traffic may introduce pollutants and municipal and industrial wastes can have a serious impact on the fishery. Industrial pressures on the coastal estuary are much more pronounced than in contained freshwater lakes.

Saltwater intrusion significantly affects crappie and weather is a prime mover of the 'salt.' Strong winds, extremely high or low barometric pressures and rain runoff alone or in combination can move the brackish buffer between the fresh and salt water around. Drought is conducive to saltwater intrusion, just as heavy showers and flooding freshens up the estuary.

Acid And Alkaline

Actually, most freshwater lakes are acidic (pH) and have a salt content. Up to a tolerable range (about 7.8 or so), the higher the pH in a lake, the better the crappie fishing. The crappie is fairly well suited for brackish waters.

Crappie feed more in brackish water than in fresh due to a greater metabolism at the higher pH level. The more extreme salt content is constantly draining from their body tissue and, to replenish it, crappie have to work harder and eat more. Since the forage intake goes into maintaining body fluids, crappie seldom grow to state record proportions in coastal waters.

Many brackish water estuaries have very short tributaries and the drainage consists primarily of low marsh lands. Many tidal-influenced rivers are stained mahogany by the tannic acid from cypress, mangrove and other swamp vegetation. Water from sawgrass marshes with few trees generally is not quite as dark, however.

Tidal waters can be very clear and, as a result, crappie fishing can be slow during midday in such areas. Many of the estuaries in the South are of this character, and those off the beaten path can provide almost some unbelievable stringers of panfish.

STATE BRACKISH WATER CRAPPIE FISHING	
STATE	COASTAL WATERS
Texas	Sabine, Neches and Colorado Rivers
Louisiana	Atchafalaya Basin, Pearl and Mississippi Rivers
Mississippi	Jorda, Pearl and Pascagoula Rivers
Alabama	Mobile Delta Tributaries
Florida	Apalachicola, Homosassa, Suwannee, Nassau, St. Johns, St. Mary and Everglades Tributaries
Georgia	St. Mary, Altamaha, Ogeechee, Satilla and Savannah Rivers
South Carolina	Combahee, Waccamaw, Santee and Cooper Rivers
North Carolina	Currituck Sound, Chowan, Neuse and Pamlico Rivers
Virginia	Rappahannock, Potomac and James Rivers
Maryland	Pokomokee River
The Others	The Northeast Atlantic States have few available. California has some crappie fishing in the Sacramento River.

Access can also be difficult to many other coastal estuaries, but some boat ramps are usually available on the main tributaries. A 30 or 40-minute boat ride may then be necessary to reach the better speck fishing, but most will consider the time invested well worth it. The tides may need to be timed just right for launching the boat, as well as for fishing.

The crappie fishing in the tidal estuary depends primarily on the condition of the water in the marshes and swamps, and in the tributaries that feed the coast. The brackish water ecosystem is a delicately-balanced one in which some crappie have found a home.

Chapter 22

TOURNAMENT PREPARATION

"The first thing we do to prepare for a tournament is get a topographical map of the lake and then study the patterns of the season," says David Stancil. "Then we look for shallow coves and backs of creeks where the best change in elevation occurs. In May and June, for example, we'll look for deep water breaklines and dropoffs near river channels and points that touch creek bends on the map. We then have located the exact spots on that map that we want to fish."

Stancil and partner Mike Howard are one of approximately 50 teams that are regulars on the crappie tournament trail. They fish 10 to 15 events each spring, and preparation for each is an important part of most all of the "touring" tournaments participants. Stancil and Howard are two multiple-Classic contestants that are aiming for fame and glory on the crappie tournament circuit.

The twosome from Oxford, Alabama, won a U.S. Crappie Association National title on Lake Russell and finished first in the Crappiethon West Point Lake event in Georgia. Stancil and Howard normally place in more than half of the tournaments they competed in each year.

143

"The main thing a good tournament angler has to do is learn how to pattern crappie," says Stancil. "Establish a pattern and stick with it."

"The secret to catching crappie during early summer, when the major crappie Classics are held, is finding a breakline with cover close to the river," Howard explains. "You should locate several such areas, because not all will hold fish. The breaklines are where the larger crappie are generally located. We could go out and catch probably 100 fish off the bridge columns, but they are 1/4 pound fish, and you are not going to win a tournament with them."

"A major aspect to our planning for a tournament is that we read magazine articles about the tournament lake," says Stancil. "The local reports in the various newspapers and magazines have a lot of valuable information. Just knowing whether the fish have recently been caught upriver or downriver, the water clarity and temperature will help to develop a plan."

Information Log

Another important part of their strategy is keeping a log of their activities and those of the winners of each tournament on various lakes. They record the water temperature, clarity of water, color of jigs that produced best, where they caught their fish and how, and if they didn't win the event, where and how the winners did. When the tournament rolls around the following year, they consult their log for appropriate valuable information.

Tournament fishermen that don't keep up with the fishing on a variety of lakes won't usually fare well in a major event like a crappie Classic, according to Stancil. To compete there, the anglers should be able to do well on different lakes that they haven't seen before. Many "Classic" contestants, though, have only fished their home lakes and the structure they put out.

"Fishing just a home lake hinders you," says Stancil. "We go to different lakes, do our homework, study the water, but on our home lake, we know where the fish are supposed to be. We try to fish those areas where they should be, and we get beat. On

Tournament fishermen who don't keep up with the fishing on a variety of lakes won't usually fare well in a major event like a crappie Classic. To compete, anglers should be able to do well on different lakes that they haven't seen before.

the distant tournaments, we try to find fish, instead of putting them in a favorite spot.''

For a recent major Classic, the two traveled to Clemson, South Carolina, in April to talk with some local bait and tackle shops and marinas. They wanted to gather information on how the spawn was going, what the crappie were hitting and what kind of structures the fish were using. The two found out where the water with the most clarity and most color was and other basic lake facts.

''You can't listen to every marina operator and then go hunt their fish,'' Howard warns. ''You'll end up not catching any fish. You'll be hunting things that you will never find.''

''We really just wanted to know what part of the lake produces fish,'' adds Stancil. ''When they are shallow, everybody can catch them, and we know those spots won't produce one month later. We don't listen to their specific spots, because we won't catch fish there. We go out and find our own spots.''

Pre-Fishing And Scouting
The two recommend pre-fishing every tournament possible. Stancil has a crappie master boat rigged just for catching that species. It is set up to troll up to 16 jigs at one time. Once on

145

the water, they first scout out the area with their depthfinder, and then, when fish are seen on the electronics, they drop their lures and begin a trolling pass.

During the tournament practice day, they normally have to check out five spots to find two that produce. If they catch fish in the first five minutes from a spot selected, they have to protect the spot by fishing without hooks on their jigs. They don't want to catch a crappie in front of other contestants, and there are often plenty around. When there are 100 or 200 boats fishing a big tournament, the best locations have to remain a secret.

With the kind of money riding on the line that a Crappie Classic tournament win may net, you can't let other contestants see you catching fish on your number one spot or tell them about catching fish when you come in. Howard and Stancil always tell others that they caught no fish in practice.

The evening before the tournament, after the practice day, the team once again goes over the map and analyzes the spots that held fish that day. They'll discuss which one to go to first and whether or not other contestants might fish the same spots that they have located. Howard and Stancil make a judgment on the best spot to win the tournament and decide how many hours to spend on each site during the event.

Bobby Martin and Alan Padgett are possibly the most well-known crappie anglers in the nation. Their tournament accomplishments are lengthy. Like most top finishers, they study maps and talk to locals prior to the event. During a Classic on Hartwell Lake, Martin and Padgett found several productive looking spots not too far from the launching point, on a lake map. On such a large lake, it is time consuming to travel long distances to a spot.

"The first thing we do is get a map of the lake to find out as much as we can about it," says Padgett. "Then, we try to talk to people around the lake to find out what the fish are doing, whether they are in a pre-spawn or bedding situation. The day before the Classic, for example, Padgett and Martin drove

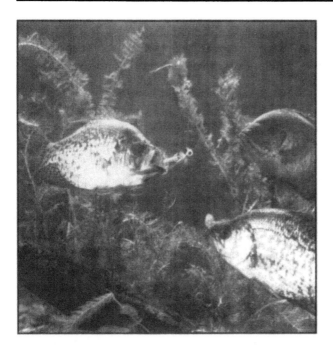

Scouting before the tournament will help discover the best crappie hangouts.

around the lake and talked to several marina operators and other locals.

"We got a lot of information at the marinas, like the crappie had already spawned, but we also got some bad information," he cautions. "We were told by one of the first people we talked with that the water temperature was lower than it was. We thought then that maybe some of the crappie hadn't spawned, but once we got on the lake in practice we found a higher temperature."

"We had to really change what we thought we were going to do on practice day," he continued. "We thought, with the initial low temperature report, that some fish might be in shallower water. We had to adapt to the right conditions on practice day."

During a regular event, they normally do more pre-fishing to determine such lake characteristics. In the Classic, they fished creek channels, points and dropoffs, as they usually do, and found fish. At other events, the twosome spends two or three days of pre-fishing. For each of their 15 tournaments a year, the team practices with existing line that they have on their reels. Then, Martin and Padgett put new line on all the reels the evening before the event. Such preparation has worked for them.

Classic Preparation

Bobby Jacobs and Ellis Arthur won a Crappiethon Classic a few years back in an area that they were relegated to when their boat broke down. They fished around utility tower obstacles, tying up to the structures and drifting around them. They caught enough fish to win the event. In another year, after double-qualifying by finishing first in a Lake Norman, North Carolina tournament and then second in a Lake Kerr, North Carolina event, they planned on a more strategic approach to the Classic.

Their Classic preparation plans included looking over a map of Lake Hartwell and selecting main creek channel areas that might hold fish. They chose five spots to check on practice day and found crappie in all areas. Another important part of their strategy for the big event was to switch from 10 pound test line down to six, due to the relatively clear water in Hartwell.

Jocobs and Arthur caught larger fish on one particular spot during practice and decided to start off there the morning of the Classic. Five baits attracted crappie at one time on their first trolling pass over the area, and they stayed in that location all day. Both Bette's jigs and live minnows hung off the 14 B&M poles. Each attracted several crappie with the jigs slightly out-producing the live bait. The Southeast Virginia men were able to stick to their strategic approach for the Classic that year. And, it worked. They brought in 20.82 pounds of crappie and finished a little less than three pounds out in third place.

These six expert crappie anglers place a lot of value in planning the right approach for a tournament. They finish very high in most events and credit proper preparation for their success.

BASS SERIES LIBRARY
by Larry Larsen

(BSL1) FOLLOW THE FORAGE - BASS/PREY RELATIONSHIP - Learn how to determine dominant forage in a body of water and catch more bass!

(BSL2) VOL. 2 BETTER BASS ANGLING TECHNIQUES - Learn why one lure or bait is more successful than others and how to use each lure under varying conditions.

(BSL3) BASS PRO STRATEGIES - Professional fishermen know how changes in pH, water level, temperature and color affect bass fishing, and they know how to adapt to weather and topographical variations. Learn from their experience.

(BSL4) BASS LURES - TRICKS & TECHNIQUES - When bass become accustomed to the same artificials and presentations seen over and over again, they become harder to catch. You will learn how to modify your lures and rigs and how to develop new presentation and retrieve methods to spark the interest of largemouth!

HAVE THEM ALL!

"Larry, I'm ordering one book to give a friend for his birthday and your two new ones. I have all the BASS SERIES LIBRARY except one, otherwise I would have ordered an autographed set. I have followed your writings for years and consider them the best of the best!"
J. Vinson, Cataula, GA

(BSL5) SHALLOW WATER BASS - Bass spend 90% of their time in waters less than 15 feet deep. Learn productive new tactics that you can apply in marshes, estuaries, reservoirs, lakes, creeks and small ponds, and you'll triple your results!

(BSL6) BASS FISHING FACTS - Learn why and how bass behave during pre- and post-spawn, how they utilize their senses when active and how they respond to their environment, and you'll increase your bass angling success!

(BSL7) TROPHY BASS - If you're more interested in wrestling with one or two monster largemouth than with a "panful" of yearlings, then learn what techniques and locations will improve your chances.

TWO TROPHIES!

"By using your techniques and reading your Bass Series Library of books, I was able to catch the two biggest bass I've ever caught!"
B. Conley, Cromwell, IN

(BSL8) ANGLER'S GUIDE TO BASS PATTERNS - Catch bass every time out by learning how to develop a productive pattern quickly and effectively. "Bass Patterns" is a reference source for all anglers, regardless of where they live or their skill level. Learn how to choose the right lure, presentation and habitat under various weather and environmental conditions!

(BSL9) BASS GUIDE TIPS - Learn secret techniques known only in a certain region or state that often work in waters all around the country. It's this new approach that usually results in excellent bass angling success. Learn how to apply what the country's top guides know!

Nine Great Volumes To Help You Catch More and Larger Bass!

(LB1) LARRY LARSEN ON BASS TACTICS

is the ultimate "how-to" book that focuses on proven productive methods. **Hundreds of highlighted tips and drawings in our LARSEN ON BASS SERIES explain how you**

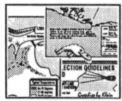

can catch more and larger bass in waters all around the country. This reference source by America's best known bass fishing writer will be invaluable to both the avid novice and expert angler!

(PF1) PEACOCK BASS EXPLOSIONS! by Larry Larsen

A must read for those anglers who are interested in catching the world's most exciting fresh water fish! Detailed tips, trip planning and tactics for peacocks in South Florida, Venezuela, Brazil, Puerto Rico, Hawaii and other destinations. This book explores the most effective tactics to take the aggressive peacock bass. You'll learn how to catch

more and larger fish using the valuable information from the author and expert angler, a four-time peacock bass world-record holder. It's the first comprehensive discussion on this wild and colorful fish.

BASS WATERS GUIDE SERIES by Larry Larsen

The most productive bass waters are described in this multi-volume series, including boat ramps, seasonal tactics, water characteristics and more. Numerous maps and photos detail specific locations.

(BW1) GUIDE TO NORTH FLORIDA BASS WATERS - Covers from Orange Lake north and west. Includes Lakes Lochloosa, Talquin and Seminole, the St. Johns, Nassau, Suwannee and Apalachicola Rivers; Newnans Lake, St. Mary's River, Juniper Lake, Ortega River, Lake Jackson, Deer Point Lake, Panhandle Mill Ponds and many more!

(BW2) GUIDE TO CENTRAL FLORIDA BASS WATERS - Covers from Tampa/Orlando to Palatka. Includes Lakes George, Rodman, Monroe, Tarpon and the Harris Chain, the St. Johns, Oklawaha and Withlacoochee Rivers, the Ocala Forest, Crystal River, Hillsborough River, Conway Chain, Homosassa River,

Lake Minneola, Lake Weir, Lake Hart, Spring Runs and many more!

(BW3) GUIDE TO SOUTH FLORIDA BASS WATERS - Covers from I-4 to the Everglades. Includes Lakes Tohopekaliga, Kissimmee, Okeechobee, Poinsett, Tenoroc and Blue Cypress, the Winter Haven Chain, Fellsmere Farm 13. Caloosahatchee River, Lake June-in-Winter, the Everglades, Lake Istokpoga, Peace River, Crooked Lake, Lake Osborne, St. Lucie Canal, Shell Creek, Lake Marian, Lake Pierce, Webb Lake and many more!

OUTDOOR TRAVEL SERIES
by Larry Larsen and M. Timothy O'Keefe
Candid guides on the best charters, time of the year, and other recommendations that can make your next fishing and/or diving trip much more enjoyable.

(OT1) FISH & DIVE THE CARIBBEAN - Vol. 1 Northern Caribbean, including Cozumel, Cayman Islands, Bahamas, Jamaica, Virgin Islands. Required reading for fishing and diving enthusiasts who want to know the most cost-effective means to enjoy these and other Caribbean islands.

(OT3) FISH & DIVE FLORIDA & The Keys - Where and how to plan a vacation to America's most popular fishing and diving destination. Features include artificial reef loran numbers; freshwater springs/caves; coral reefs/barrier islands; gulf stream/passes; inshore flats/channels; and back country estuaries.

> ### BEST BOOK CONTENT!
> *"Fish & Dive the Caribbean" was a finalist in the Best Book Content Category of the National Association of Independent Publishers (NAIP). Over 500 books were submitted by publishers including Simon & Schuster and Turner Publishing. Said the judges "An excellent source book with invaluable instructions. Written by two nationally-known experts who, indeed, know what vacationing can be!"*

DIVING SERIES by M. Timothy O'Keefe

(DL1) DIVING TO ADVENTURE shows how to get started in underwater photography, how to use current to your advantage, how to avoid seasickness, how to dive safely after dark, and how to plan a dive vacation, including live-aboard diving.

(DL2) MANATEES - OUR VANISHING MERMAIDS is an in-depth overview of nature's strangest-looking, gentlest animals. They're among America's most endangered mammals. The book covers where to see manatees while diving, why they may be living fossils, their unique life cycle, and much more.

UNCLE HOMER'S OUTDOOR CHUCKLE BOOK
by Homer Circle, Fishing Editor, Sports Afield

(OC1) In his inimitable humorous style, "Uncle Homer" relates jokes, tales, personal anecdotes and experiences covering several decades in the outdoors. These stories, memories and moments will bring grins, chuckles and deep down belly laughs as you wend your way through the folksy copy and cartoons. If you appreciate the lighter side of life, this book is a must!

OUTDOOR ADVENTURE LIBRARY
by Vin T. Sparano, Editor-in-Chief, Outdoor Life

(OA1) HUNTING DANGEROUS GAME - Live the adventure of hunting those dangerous animals that hunt back! Track a rogue elephant, survive a grizzly attack, and face a charging Cape buffalo. These classic tales will make you very nervous next time you're in the woods!

> ### KEEP ME UPDATED!
> *"I would like to get on your mailing list. I really enjoy your books!"*
> G. Granger, Cypress, CA

(OA2) GAME BIRDS & GUN DOGS - A unique collection of tales about hunters, their dogs and the upland game and waterfowl they hunt. You will read about good gun dogs and heart-breaking dogs, but never about bad dogs, because there's no such animal.

COASTAL FISHING GUIDES
by Frank Sargeant

A unique "where-to" series of detailed secret spots for Florida's finest saltwater fishing. These guide books describe hundreds of little-known honeyholes and exactly how to fish them. Prime seasons, baits and lures, marinas and dozens of detailed maps of the prime spots are included. The comprehensive index helps the reader to further pinpoint productive areas and tactics. Over $160 worth of personally-marked NOAA charts in the two books.

(FG1) FRANK SARGEANT'S SECRET SPOTS Tampa Bay to Cedar Key Covers Hillsborough River and Davis Island through the Manatee River, Mullet Key and the Suwannee River.

(FG2) FRANK SARGEANT'S SECRET SPOTS Southwest Florida Covers from Sarasota Bay to Marco.

INSHORE SERIES
by Frank Sargeant

(IL1) THE SNOOK BOOK-"Must" reading for anyone who loves the pursuit of this unique sub-tropic species. Every aspect of how you can find and catch big snook is covered, in all seasons and all waters where snook are found.

(IL2) THE REDFISH BOOK-Packed with expertise from the nation's leading redfish anglers and guides, this book covers every aspect of finding and fooling giant reds. You'll learn secret techniques revealed for the first time. After reading this informative book, you'll catch more redfish on your next trip!

(IL3) THE TARPON BOOK-Find and catch the wily "silver king" along the Gulf Coast, north through the mid-Atlantic, and south along Central and South American coastlines. Numerous experts share their most productive techniques.

(IL4) THE TROUT BOOK -Jammed with tips from the nation's leading trout guides and light tackle anglers. For both the old salt and the rank amateur who pursue the spotted weakfish, or seatrout, throughout the coastal waters of the Gulf and Atlantic.

HUNTING LIBRARY
by John E. Phillips

(DH1) MASTERS' SECRETS OF DEER HUNTING - Increase your deer hunting success by learning from the masters of the sport. New information on tactics and strategies is included in this book, the most comprehensive of its kind.

(DH2) THE SCIENCE OF DEER HUNTING Covers why, where and when a deer moves and deer behavior. Find the answers to many of the toughest deer hunting problems a sportsman ever encounters!

(DH3) MASTERS' SECRETS OF BOW-HUNTING DEER - Learn the skills required to take more bucks with a bow, even during gun season. A must read for those who walk into the woods with a strong bow and a swift shaft.

(TH1) MASTERS' SECRETS OF TURKEY HUNTING - Masters of the sport have solved some of the most difficult problems you can encounter while hunting wily longbeards with bows, blackpowder guns and shotguns. Learn the 10 deadly sins of turkey hunting.

> **RECOMMENDATION!**
> *"Masters' Secrets of Turkey Hunting is one of the best books around. If you're looking for a good turkey book, buy it!"*
> J. Spencer, Stuttgart Daily Leader, AR
>
> **NO BRAGGIN'!**
> *"From anyone else Masters' Secrets of Deer Hunting would be bragging and unbelievable. But not with John Phillips, he's paid his dues!"* F. Snare, Brookville Star, OH

(BP1) BLACKPOWDER HUNTING SECRETS - Learn how to take more game during and after the season with black powder guns. If you've been hunting with black powder for years, this book will teach you better tactics to use throughout the year.

FISHING LIBRARY

(CF1) MASTERS' SECRETS OF CRAPPIE FISHING by John E. Phillips Learn how to make crappie start biting again once they have stopped, select the best jig color, find crappie in a cold front, through the ice, or in 100-degree heat. Unusual, productive crappie fishing techniques are included.

(CF2) CRAPPIE TACTICS by Larry Larsen - Whether you are a beginner or a seasoned crappie fisherman, this book will improve your catch! The book includes some basics for fun fishing, advanced techniques for year 'round crappie and tournament preparation.

> **CRAPPIE COUP!**
> *"After reading your crappie book, I'm ready to overthrow the 'crappie king' at my lakeside housing development!"*
> R. Knorr, Haines City, FL

(CF3) MASTERS' SECRETS OF CATFISHING by John E. Phillips is your best guide to catching the best-tasting, elusive cats. If you want to know the best time of the year, the most productive places and which states to fish in your pursuit of Mr. Whiskers, then this book is for you. Special features include how to find and take monster cats, what baits to use and when, how to find a tailrace groove and more strategies for rivers or lakes.

INDEX

A

acid rain   119
Altamaha River   91
analysis, lake   101-106
Atchafalaya Basin   93, 96

B

bait   13-18
Barkley Lake   91
boat houses   74
bobbers   25-28
brackish waters   136-142
Braunig Reservoir   91
bridges   47
brush piles   47, 71
buoys   121-128

C

Calaveras Reservoir   91
catch and release   49-52
chubsuckers   76
clinch knot   30
coastal estuaries   137
Color-C-Lector   108, 113

cooling reservoir   87
crankbaits   17
Crappie Classic   146
Crappiethon   143
Crescent Lake   108

D

Dardanelle impoundment   91
depth finder   82, 107
docks   73-78

E

East Bay   135
electronics   107-112
equipment   19-24

F

Fayette Reservoir   91
floating docks   47
floats   26
Florida waters   46
flyfishing   23
"Follow The Forage For Better
    Bass Angling"   47
forage   60

G

Global Positioning
        Systems 111
good spots 57-60
grass 61-66

H

Harris Chain of Lakes   77
Herrington Lake   91
hooks   25-28

J

jig colors   14

L

Lake Anna   91
Lake Griffin   61
Lake Hartwell   146, 148
Lake Kerr   148
Lake Monticello   91
Lake Norman   91, 148
Lake Russell   143
Lake Sinclair   91
Lake Welsh   91
Lay Lake   91
LCR   98
line   29-34
live bait   25
Loran   111
lures   13-18
    colors   14

M

Map and Research
        Reports   102
marker buoys   122-128
marsh fishing   93-100
minnows   26, 40, 76
Masters' Secrets of
        Crappie Fishing   154
monofilament line   29
mount   53-56
    fiberglass   55
    skin mounts   55
    trophy   49, 53

N

natural markers   124
Neely Henry Lake   91
nuclear power plant   87

P

pH   38, 40, 42, 87,
        92, 113-120
piers   47, 73-78
pits   79-86
potguts   76
power plant reservoirs   87-92

R

reels   19-24
Resource Directory   47, 149
rock formations   71
rods   19-24

S

San Jacinto River   140
scent patterns   133
scent products   129-134
shiners   76
skirts   14
soft baits   132
sonar
   see electronics
Sooner Lake   91
spawn   35-42, 58, 69, 138
spool memory   32
structure   47, 67-72
summer tactics   43-48

T

Tenoroc Fish Management
      Area   79
tidal-influence   135-142
Toledo Bend   57
topographical map   102, 112
tournament   143
   preparation   143-147
Trinity River   139
trophy   49, 53
Turtle Creek Reservoir   35

U

U.S. Crappie Association   143
ultralight rods   23

W

Watts Bar Lake   91
weed beds   47
West Point Lake   143

Breinigsville, PA USA
20 June 2010
240141BV00001BA/4/P